PAPER CONCERT

Paper Concert

A Conversation in the Round

Amy Wright

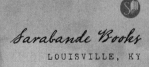

Sarabande Books
LOUISVILLE, KY

Publisher's Cataloging-In-Publication Data
(Prepared by The Donohue Group, Inc.)

Names: Wright, Amy, 1975– author.
Title: Paper concert : a conversation in the round / Amy Wright.
Description: Louisville, KY : Sarabande Books, 2021
Identifiers: ISBN 9781946448804 (paperback) | ISBN 9781946448811 (e-book)
Subjects: LCSH: Authors, American—21st century—Interviews.
American literature—21st century. | Authorship. | Imagination.
BISAC: LITERARY COLLECTIONS / Essays. | LITERARY COLLECTIONS / Interviews.
LITERARY COLLECTIONS / Women Authors. | LITERARY COLLECTIONS /
American / General. | LCGFT: Interviews. | Essays.
Classification: LCC PS135 .W75 2021 (print) | LCC PS135 (e-book)
DDC 810.9/006—dc23

Cover and interior design by Alban Fischer
Cover image: *Mycorrhizal Fungi* by Sir David Read
Printed in Canada.
This book is printed on acid-free paper.
Sarabande Books is a nonprofit literary organization.

This project is supported in part by an award from the National Endowment
for the Arts. The Kentucky Arts Council, the state arts agency,
supports Sarabande Books with state tax dollars and federal
funding from the National Endowment for the Arts.

For my students, who teach me how to ask

CONTENTS

Perhaps my writing career began when I asked my first question.... Or sooner. Buddha said in this life we look for our fingerprints from our other lives.

—IRA SUKRUNGRUANG

I.

I Don't Mean that Swans Are Humane

OUTSIDE THE WINDOW by my writing desk grows a fringe tree. For years prior to acquiring this view I lived in apartments, my desk turned toward a wall, my ears plugged against the cries of sirens, so this fleecy white foliage often charms my gaze between taps on the keyboard. One day, in late summer, I noticed a strand of spiderweb blowing from a high branch. Sunlight snagged the silk just right, so it glistened like a silver hair before vanishing into the distance. It was caught on something, but there was nothing for it to reach in that direction except the roof of my house, over fifteen feet away. I stood to investigate and saw that the line connected to the eave over a chasm hundreds of times the length of a large spider. The silk was slack to accommodate wind, but, like Philippe Petit's tightrope between the Twin Towers, it spanned a space that was both terrifying and laughable. I imagined that the spider realized her folly after stringing the anchor line and gave up, exhausted, but I admired the ambition; a web that broad could have netted dragonflies from the Carboniferous period with their three-foot wingspans. I wondered if the spider embodied some ancient memory of that era, or just had a tremendous appetite. I returned to my desk to work.

Later that morning, I looked again and saw her, red-bodied and bulbous, sitting at the center of a web she had strung beneath that vast center line that shone like an eye. She had managed it! She was mad! I went outside and photographed her triumph.

I could not fathom the engineering. The distance between the tree and roof looked impossible to leap. Even if she had ballooned across the gulf, carried by wind, spinning midair, that thread would have had to bear her weight as she reinforced it. She could have made the pilgrimage on the ground and lifted the cable, but it would have stuck on a grass blade and torn. I puzzled over the logistics, then let it become a metaphor: an essayist in miniature, the spider had spun a line as tenuous as the one that starts the fabric of an idea.

This essay began eleven years ago with a question. I was thirty-two. I had just moved to Tennessee from Colorado. I did not know how to ask the question yet, since it embarrassed me that I did not know the answer, but I was now editing a magazine that dared me to stage an attempt. The question was one I had spun for decades, sturdy enough that a web of other questions might be strung from it. It first formed in my mind on the oatmeal-colored carpet of my girlhood bedroom, but I had asked it so many times since then that I was no longer sure of the words I used, only of the sentiment: *What am I?*

"The self is a mirror facing a mirror in which clouds arise," my friend Alan said years later, after he spent a month in the Himalayas watching Mount Everest and Annapurna pull clouds from the air like handkerchiefs. His definition explained why the question sustained my interest: it wasn't a search for personal identity but for the origins of the conflict at the heart of being.

Even as a child, I was clear that there was no singular authority on anything. Your mother would tell you one thing, your grandfather another. Teachers, friends, and your great-aunt Edna from Pennsylvania all advised different things. The best a self-interested kid could do was lie, I determined, prepared to shape a thousand faces to meet the faces that I met—before I got caught and had to swear one hundred times in writing not to do that again. Afterward, I decided I needed a system. If I could rank and file information, I could apply it as befitted each situation to maximize rewards and reduce punishment. It would be a survival manual more valuable than instructions to escape quicksand, because it would include that guidance, too. It would note the world's best ketchup (Annie's), and include a chart of heaven, the highest goal I could imagine at the time thanks to Emily Dickinson's poem "I Never Saw a Moor."

This essay is, as is this book, such a system, meaning a) a scheme, b) a comprehensive and methodically arranged survey of a subject, and c) a set of persons working together as parts of an interconnecting network. The methodology, as personal as a gambler's system for placing bets, derives from fear. If as a child I feared being unloved, shunned, targeted, or ignored, as an adult I fear those things and more. I fear the environmental havoc we are wreaking on this planet with the profligate burning of fossil fuels. I fear the food crisis to come when the global population bulges to ten billion and collapses the Western agricultural model. I fear delusion. I fear readers too tired to protest class divides. I fear the mind that seeks authority, hunts for argument like fresh meat but swears it wants peace. I fear failing to ask the question able to dispel the illusion that I am somehow separate from the context I reflect.

The essaying goes on, but this essay anchors a central thread of dialogue over a dizzying divide. It weaves a decade-plus's worth of questions and answers from a range of discussions I've had with artists, activists, scientists, philosophers, physicians, priests, musicians, and other representatives of the human population. Some of them are famous, some will be, some should be—but all of them refract the light of the unknowable mystery of the self. Sometimes they turned the tables and interviewed me, carrying our conversation into the realm of true dialogue. It was always dialogue I sought—of the kind Dickinson inspired, across time and space—from the Greek *dia logos,* the reason we come together.

Although continuous within me, the questions were scattered across media, until one afternoon, energized by a yoga set, I copied some forty interviews into one document and reread them. I had put various experts, issues, and insights into conversation, but only with myself. The collective didn't exist in that patchwork document but hung in the air over it, from which I began to pull a thread of whole cloth. I strung additional strands from that center line, which was wide enough, I hoped, to provision me for life: the latticework of an internal dialogue made external.

I was pretty free as a kid. My family lived on a farm in the Blue Ridge Mountains surrounded by creeks, woods, wildlife, abandoned sheds, and cattle trucks with the keys still in them. I did not have to direct myself toward anyone else's expectations for hours at a time. Those hours, too, were an essay, a foray into life's experiment, and they taught me that research always begins and ends in the field.

When in your life have you felt the freest?

Michael Martone: When I was trapped on an island. The island was Serifos, a Greek island, said to be the home of Perseus. The strange rock formation on the ridges of the mountains was all that was left of his enemies frozen there when he aimed Medusa's head at them. It was late season, September, and the Meltemi was blowing from the north. I was staying in a house with no running water in the old town at the top of the mountain. Each morning, I would look down at the harbor and watch the sailboats attempt to leave the port, but they could not round the point. They stalled, attempting to reach and tack into that wind. I realized, suddenly, that even if I had to be somewhere else there was no way I was going to get there. I had that same feeling when, more recently, I totaled my car going seventy, plowing into a bridge abutment. I lost control oversteering, and time, as we know, slowed. And that feeling of great calm came over me, a freedom derived from helplessness. The moment when I was most helpless, I felt most free. To control is to roll against, and that, I think, is a kind of self-generated prison. The secret is to roll with.

•••••••••••

If you could control anything what would it be?

Kristina Marie Darling: I would be in control of my repressed desires. Sometimes, after waking from a strange dream, I imagine the conscious mind as a little door leading into the wilderness.

············

What are some of your structural models for composing an essay?

Kat Meads: In her preface to *Rock, Water, Wild,* Nancy Lord tells readers the chapters ahead are "*essays* in the original meaning of the word—that is, *attempts* to learn, to discover, to wander around in ideas as I try to reach some understandings." (The italics are hers.) I feel similarly. Particularly with regard to the "wander around" aspect.

············

In *Zoologies*, while observing cones of sand and gravel sculpted into floral patterns by desert leafcutter ants, you wonder if art is a biological need. Has a work of art ever served a biological function for you?

Alison Hawthorne Deming: That's not quite what I mean by art serving a biological need. Just as the ants' flower cones are an artifact of their foraging that reveals the underlying imperative in nature toward pattern and form, so does art-making reveal this need in our makeup. We have a biological need to take in food and turn it into energy. Perhaps we have a need to take in experience, with all its disorder and randomness, and turn it into form and pattern, which is art (and also science!). As I see it, our artistic drive reflects the imperative toward form that shapes all of nature and so is part of our biological heritage.

•••••••••••

Does all art equally exemplify an imperative toward form, or do particular works come to mind?

Alison Hawthorne Deming: When I think of the received poetic forms—sonnet, villanelle, sestina, and such—they remind me of the variety in leaf or flower form, each quite distinct and yet following the inventive rules of its kind. When I think of the abstract expressionist paintings of de Kooning and Pollock and Rothko, I think these are perfectly matched with the twentieth century's interest in the theory of relativity and quantum dynamics—imprecise and yet speaking of an underlying truth, an imperative toward form and the dissolution of form. Stravinsky said, if you give me form, you give me freedom. All art teeters on the edge of that paradox.

•••••••••••

You write that ultimately "it's not so much our technology, but what we believe, that will determine our fate" as a species. What do you believe?

Tim Flannery: I believe that we're in the midst of a great transition, and that it is probably the moment of greatest peril in the human journey so far simply because we are in the same boat now. The whole world is coalescing into one single unit, and the way we handle climate change will determine whether we as a species adapt and survive into the future.

•••••••••••

How did you craft a narrative for *The Tribal Knot*, a multi-generational memoir that braids stories of your family across distance and decades? And what gave you the courage to undertake such a project?

Rebecca McClanahan: Courage? Is it courage when you have no idea of what's ahead of you? Because I had no idea where the trail would lead. I've never had an idea where any writing adventure might lead; if I did, I probably would hang back like the Cowardly Lion. I just plunged in because I was so fascinated by the letters and documents and artifacts, and later by the oral histories and interviews, that I could not have stopped even had I wanted to. I was hooked. As for the form, it developed over a long period of trial and error. But once I discovered the ancestral hair-weaving detail—through one of my interviews—that image helped me see that the narrative would be shaped at least partly by interwoven histories. I also opted for fairly straightforward chronology, to help the reader move through time with me.

••••••••••••

In your essay "Meditations in the Hut," you describe reading as "a form of experience" that happens "simultaneously in the author's mind and the reader's mind with only the thin printed page as conduit between." How does the interview dynamic contribute to the exchange of energy, information, beauty, wisdom?

Dan Beachy-Quick: Most fundamentally, I suppose, it makes available to others something usually denied them—access to thinking as it occurs in the moment of reaction that real dialogue requires. It seems to offer, ideally, a profound kind of trespass, an overhearing, in which the actual importance of two people talking together exists not in the conversation itself, but rather in the intimacy only trespass allows: a glance, a glimpse, a listening-in that feels worthy exactly because it doesn't initially belong to you at all. As for the two doing the interview together, it keeps in the air and active what could otherwise be static, it adds a conversation to a reading, and it refuses the page as the lone thinker's solitary refuge, forcing the page to speak back into the world as a still-forming rather than an already-formed thing.

....

How does the essay follow, or resist following, your mind on the page?

Jericho Parms: Ideas shape movement. Observations shape movement. Research shapes movement, too.

I think of the relationship between research and writing as a merry-go-round where there is both vertical motion and horizontal motion. Information that exists in the world at large can propel a piece while thoughts and images in my own mind bob along, rising and deepening at points. Or vice versa. And perhaps, like a merry-go-around, an essay might not ever arrive somewhere but seek instead to journey through texture and sounds, patterns and silences—language—until we step off the ride, slightly dizzy or seeing stars, with some sense of meaning.

That said, inevitably some essays resist, or rather insist, on cutting a separate path. In those moments it's up to me to follow. Often eagerly, on occasion, dragging my feet like a child—but childlike, too, in my own willingness to be awed, inspired to imagine, led by curiosity, *shaped* by whatever happens upon the page.

....

In "On Form," you describe an essayist's task of "recording, recording, recording." I know you are a conscientious watcher, so you must have noticed your decisions to leave out certain information. In "Autopsy Report," for example, you eliminate the backstory that brings you to the twelve naked male bodies on dissecting tables. "Stay with me," you say in another essay. "Events will fit themselves to themselves." Is this your trust in the reader to hold lightly the reins of narrative, or is there a private methodology to the missing?

Lia Purpura: This is a spectacular question and gets at the heart of some complicated issues about aesthetics, creating, and the act of reflecting on one's own work. I am *aware*, of course, of the writer-as-shaping-force, but I have a hard time talking about my *method*—I don't want to sound dumb or withholding in any way, but here's the truth: I try not to think too hard about how I do what I do. I guess it would be accurate to say, yes, I *do* trust the reader to hold lightly the reins of the narrative, or to be patient while an essay unfolds. I *do* believe in my reader—mysterious, distant, unknown as s/he is to me. That's the way my faith unfolds or expresses. Sometimes I feel the need to encourage or reassure the reader a little, so I do that. There's no "private methodology" at work, in terms of what's elided or foregrounded. I'm trying in each essay to be what I know of as "myself" on the page, to think and feel openly. I hope I keep getting closer and closer to that which is impossible to say. This way of proceeding is what makes it hard to teach; what am I going to say, "Just be yourself?" That's less than helpful and too opaque. People want to "get it"—readers and students alike deserve to be invited in—so I try my best to teach like a writer, to point out issues of balance and missing or overemphasized parts, to help people read closely, to help them learn how to love a piece.

....

In your mission statement for the community-based press Sona Books, you say that a publisher's job is to "keep an ear to the ground about alternative models, to listen to the quiet or quieted community members especially." Will you talk about the value of listening for what might otherwise be missed?

Jill Magi: When I think about the whole world of publishing—and I try not to do this too often!—I am sure that experimental and risky works are harder to come by. They are harder for bookstores to carry; they are not reviewed by mainstream publications or through mainstream channels, and those voices are often silenced.

I should say that I define risk in two ways: in terms of content that might be otherwise ignored, suppressed, considered *minority* in point of view, adversarial to mainstream culture, or even an intervention in what might considered *experimental*— and in terms of form, works that might play with language to the degree that in reading, we need to ask, as poet Ann Lauterbach has pointed out, "What is this text doing?" rather than "What does this mean?" I also look for works that look outside the individual experience toward macro social structures.

But I do not live my life lamenting the fact that you won't find

many of these books on the shelves at large bookstores. So be it.
We just have to work harder in more personal ways to sustain our
communities and reach out, whenever possible, and let folks know
about all the variety of literature that exists. I would rather act in
this way in the world than sit back and wait to hear from my agent
or editor on "sales figures" or where I've been scheduled to read. In
a small way, Sona Books is about this personal reach—the lively
world of personal distribution networks.

•••••••••••

What is the role of reflection in crafting a narrative?

Rebecca McClanahan: The kinds of nonfiction I like to read
require more than one or two rhetorical modes. Narrative is not
enough. Description is not enough. Onstage action is not enough.
We need a mix of modes to keep the text from becoming static.
Reflection and musing are modes that can enrich a narrative; as a
reader, I want to feel that the deeper, timeless questions are being
plumbed by the author, questions that could outlive the narrative
itself. And if I, as the author, have an insight involving that deeper
level, even one that occurs to me in the very act of writing, why
not allow that move to show up on the page?

Why not *muse?* Hold on a minute. I'm grabbing my *OED*,
Volume 10, from the shelf. I love my *OED*, all twenty heavy
volumes; great weight-lifting exercise, too. *Muse* is such a writerly
word, but I'll bet I don't really know what it means. Okay, let's see.

Of course, there are the mythological girls, figures of inspiration; and "to meditate"; well, that goes without saying. "To gaze; to wait; to murmur, grumble, complain." Hmm. "To wonder, marvel, bewilder." Bewilder: I like that. "Muse: a bagpipe." A bagpipe? Who knew? "The fruit of a plantain or banana." The plot thickens. But here's my favorite: "A fit of abstraction." Yes, a fit, indeed. And I believe I've just been seized by one.

·····   ·····   ··

In your poem "He Watches Them," the speaker, watching a tussle of birds, confesses to thinking only of himself when he reads, "Nests are tragedy waiting to happen." In that moment, the poem isolates a frame within a larger narrative. Who or what are some of your models for constructing frames?

Ellen Doré Watson: I think all art-making is about framing—freeze-framing, to allow for an intimate, layered gaze, which then gives us the insight to contextualize and acknowledge perspective, to step back far enough to see a real thing as a metaphor, and a metaphor as tangible and real. A fundamental part of craft in any art is cropping—deciding how far to zoom in or out, what's extraneous vs. what's crucial to a particular moment being explored in a particular way. And everywhere I look, I see my instructors in this....

Adrienne Rich's "Frame" comes immediately to mind. It's brilliant not only in its framing (in every sense of the word), but also in its strategy, leading the attentive reader to discoveries that are revelatory and disturbing, and which break down the frames and barriers that divide the poet from history. I also think of Robert Hass's *Sun Under Wood*, the surprising distances between the poems' starting and finishing points, and especially about the framework of "Faint Music," the way its last line echoes and underlines the path of the piece: "First an ego, and then pain, and then the singing."

....

Are there formal traditions you honor or rebel against with your paintings?

David Iacovazzi-Pau: You have to take risks when you paint, especially with portraits because portraiture has existed for a very long time. The oldest one was discovered in a cave near Angoulême that is over twenty-five thousand years old, so we have had plenty of time to work on the subject!

I don't see myself as a traditionalist even though I was trained in that manner. I embrace standards, yet I enjoy breaking them in order to push my work further. I'm not looking to make a picture-perfect painting. Edgar Allan Poe [quoting Francis Bacon] said: "There is no excellent beauty that hath not some strangeness in the proportion."

I don't rely solely on paint brushes. I sometimes use pieces of a cut-up dustpan, rags or dry pigments, among other things.

I also keep the composition as simple as possible in my portraits because I want the viewer's eyes to lock on the person and not be distracted. It's important to keep the interaction very direct.

•••••••••••

How do you feel about ketchup?

Michael Martone: I send bottles of ketchup at Christmas for presents. A brand called Red Gold is bottled in Indiana. I like the poetry in the name, the unexpected juxtaposition. And there is the implication of gold being in such a humble product. Did you see that Heinz's new label removes the pickle and the 57 varieties? They know on which side their bread is buttered or their condiment spread.

•••••••••••

When in your life have you felt the freest?

Ira Sukrungruang: Man, this question has got me spinning. Right now, the still moments when my son leans against me as we do nothing. In those moments nothing else matters. Nothing is as important. And I know it is fleeting. I know it won't last. Because he is getting older, but also because his capacity to sit still is waning by the day. So I like writing about it in poems and essays. A snapshot. A still shot.

Here is one from an essay written in letters to Bodhi titled "Letters in the Early Light of Morning": "But sometimes, when I am awake and stay awake, I do not leave the bed. Sometimes, I find you nestled against me. Holding on to my arm. My torso becomes a cave you hide in, my chest a fire that chases away any chill. In those moments, I stay. And wait the hours until you rise."

....

How do metaphors contribute to your modes of thinking?

Eric LeMay: We all think metaphorically. As essayists, it's how we come to understand what our work is and does. Lia Purpura, for example, likens her essays to miniatures, and Ander Monson likens his to hacks. In Montaigne's case, his metaphor is a monster: his essays are like "monstrous bodies [*corps monstrueux*] patched and huddled up together of diverse members, without any certain or well-ordered figure, having neither order, dependency, or proportion, but casual and framed by chance."

....

Your collection *Multiply/Divide* makes a powerful compositional statement by alternating fiction, nonfiction, and lyric essays. In your opening author's note, you identify each piece's genre, even as you question the distinction. Is there a function or goal you look to all writing to serve, beyond categorization?

Wendy S. Walters: I like to imagine myself as part of the broad tradition of African American writing, but I also think of that tradition as being part of or in conversation with writers who embrace the idea of hemisphere, whose understanding of geography moves from the top of North America to the bottom of South America. Writing through and across disciplines is not unusual among writers in Canada, Argentina, the Caribbean, Colombia, Mexico, as well as in indigenous and Native communities who attempt to reckon with deep, unresolved histories of violence. Some of the writers with vastly different perspectives who have influenced me in my thinking about this shared tradition include Jorge Luis Borges, Rosario Ferré, Rossana Reguillo, Valeria Luiselli, Tomás Rivera, Natalie Diaz, Daniel David Moses, Monique Mojica, and N. Scott Momaday.

....

What do moments of passion look like in your work?

David Huddle: Last spring my Hollins workshop voted in the topic of *heirloom* for the next week's assignment. Here's my opening paragraph:

> Throughout my childhood a wooden cabinet with odd
> punched-metal panels in its doors and shelves full of
> useless scraps and jars sat out on our back porch adjacent
> to the weekly used wringer washing machine. Long ago
> that cabinet had been carelessly painted white, but the

years of weather, along with dust from the driveway, had darkened it into a profoundly undistinguished shade of grayish brown. On an afternoon when I was about eight, it seemed logical to me to hack at that thing with a butcher knife, thereby gouging triangles of wood out of its top edge, giving it an improvised serration that seemed to me quite appealing. When my mother appeared on the porch and discovered what I'd done, she got in my face and instructed me as follows: A) If I ever played with a butcher knife again, I'd be very, very sorry; B) I had better learn to respect things that belonged to grown-ups; and C) the thing that I had just irreparably ruined was a pie press that had belonged to great-grandmother Akers, that could not be replaced, and that was—didn't I understand?!—an *heirloom*. You might think that experience would have instilled in me a lifelong respect for heirlooms. Not so. Sixty years later the very concept of *heirloom* just pisses me off.

··········

In your essay "Yom Kippur Pear," you confess a sixty-year-old memory in which you, at fourteen, break a fast with a rosy ripe bite from a Bartlett pear. You say that your confession is exceptional because it is offered without fear for your soul's fate, being at a point in your life "too far gone, too ruined, too free, for that." Is there anything left from which you have not freed yourself?

Gerald Stern: We are never free. Well, some of us might attain that. There is fear of death and sickness; there are family duties; there are responsibilities to friends and colleagues; there is work. Several poets, seeking freedom in their respective ways, have written poems attacking responsibility. I have friends who fled to mountains and valleys, who lived by their wits in San Francisco, New York, or Greece, and who felt they were free, or at least said so. Maybe freedom is a state of mind.... The pear was delicious.

....

Was it love of language, or something else, that inspired the "drops of mercy" in your poem "Swan Song"?

Gerald Stern: I would say basically that it is love of humanity that is always there with me, and certainly in "Swan Song," which started in the movement of a swan in an artificial pond and came somehow to that conclusion. I don't mean that swans are humane. (Maybe only in my poem.)

II.

The Thread that Makes the Cloth

UNTIL FOURTH GRADE, the school bus dropped me off every afternoon before a metal gate that I opened and latched behind me, and then I walked two hundred yards down my grandparents' gravel driveway. At the end of it, on an iron stand, beneath an elm tree, hung a sign that read Cove Creek Farm. As I walked, dairy cows lifted their black-and-white mottled heads to study me, chewing their cud like thoughts. At first, I feared them, or that concentrated attention, but they were so domesticated from being milked twice a day I could walk between them swinging my Strawberry Shortcake lunchbox.

One afternoon, as I made my way to the farmhouse, a rafter of wild turkeys claimed the pasture. They were fanned in an abstract formation to help them flush insects. A leader wasn't as easy to make out as in flight, although birds also shift positions midair. Each turkey looked individual in its focus, tail feathers dragging the ground like a bridal train, until they drew together to cross the drive. The alpha bird was less obvious than in cattle, who fall in step behind the lead cow who starts first to the call, first to the trough. After a series of synchronizing turns, the birds rounded like a storm front and rolled forward as one. They were a gang, a cohort, a tide. Their necks extended and retracted like lungs. It did not occur to me to think them vulnerable, since each rose nearly as high as my seven-year-old chest. Likely they would have broken like pool balls had I dared to dash toward them, but I stood still and watched them cross, remembering that turkeys could mob a person if they felt threatened.

Perhaps because at school I was learning the perks and pangs of social alliances, the birds' invisible bond seemed to offer some instruction. They seemed both oblivious of and sewn to each other, like grass blades in the wind. I tried to feel its force on my cheeks, but I was not one of them.

Later, what came to interest me about animal families were the mavericks who refused to fall in line. To farmers, outliers were a nuisance, but to an adolescent who watched beef cattle break from the herd while being rounded up and sold, outliers became heroic, a kind of animal avant-garde, first to divine signs that all is not well. Nine times out of ten, it was a calf rather than a cow with enough vim or sedition to split. I rooted for the escapees, even when they kept us in the field chasing them through lunch or supper time. In time I would lose that admiration, grow irritated along with my father at the runaways we were trying to rotate to a fresh pasture or to vaccinate against parasites. I wished their intuition keener, their wildness tame, before helping fold strays back into the herd.

I studied their nature as one might study a code. I experimented with different gestures to determine which of my actions had the most effect. I wore differently colored clothes and practiced calm. I wanted to communicate with the cattle, physically or psychically, so I could apologize, explain that we were collaborative stewards of the land, although our relationship was exploitative. We drank milk that had been pasteurized and sold to the grocer, separated yearlings from their mothers, castrated bull calves. We fattened steers to be slaughtered elsewhere, and then sat down to steak dinners. It was a raw deal at times for the doe-eyed creatures with eyelashes as long as my index finger, but worse was to wipe the fields free of them, replace their pastures with shopping centers or housing developments, and concentrate livestock on corporate farms, as was happening to most family operations. Our herd still spent the bulk of their days grazing or resting beneath shade trees with their grown heifer calves, swatting flies with their tails, and watching us head our separate ways on the dirt road.

Sometimes the cows would sniff or lick my hand over a fence, but if I reached to stroke them, they pulled away. They were a lot like people from Appalachia that way: they would rather come closer toward you than be approached. In my family, there were stories you would never hear if you asked for them straight. You had to talk around what mattered, approach from an angle, infiltrate confidences, and back off. At school, you might never know why your best friend replaced you over the weekend. Or maybe I was too proud to ask. My role models held to a form of decorum so subtle they pivoted on sidelong glances like murmurations of starlings. Outsiders characterized people from the region by the twang of accents, but missteps and overstepped bounds twanged far louder. Even a long pause could ring in your ears if you missed its implications.

At night, the wild turkeys roosted in the tops of trees surrounding my grandparents' farmhouse and our home on the other side of the shoestring branch that ran between the two. By day, they roamed a range of woods, fields, and banks that kept them out of sight, as living in the country kept me often out of sight from my friends, schoolteachers, and extended family. In town, different patterns tugged, and our close-knit family moved in other bands—as social worker, Sunday school student, insurance agent, livestock market manager, investor. Perhaps from the turkeys, perhaps from the flocks of Canada geese that touched down during their migratory routes, or the redstarts and goldfinches that came and went with seasonal berries and thistledown, I thought of that time when we scattered as practice in distinguishing ourselves and coming together.

Each evening, we rejoined with stories. We questioned other families' choices. They informed us. They altered the ways we moved together and apart, as passing hawks reroute traffic in a forest. Our circles widened but kept returning to this valley, curtained by the Blue Ridge, where buzzards rode the currents of the ridgeline, and we wound around each other, eyes on the wings for cues before we reentered the stage.

In your essay "The Weight of a Bird," you say that you used to think of connections as train cars that added up to meaning, but now you think of them "more like Virginia creeper or spaghetti. It all touches, but where one vine or strand begins and another ends is a knotted question." What are some knots you're untying lately?

Nicole Walker: I actually think I'm better at tying up than untying. Even at the end of a mass of twisted Virginia creeper, there's still the roots to deal with. One question invites another. But what questions am I making a mass out of? I'm working on a book that wants to be ecological in form as well as premise. I could write a thousand times *everything is connected*, but that just sounds like New Age speak. What I want is to say this: When you're washing your hands with antibacterial soap, the triclosan that is in that soap goes out to the water treatment plant. It doesn't reduce. It compounds in solid waste. The solid waste is trucked to the desert. The desert wind blows. And then my leap in logic and time, since the ramifications of pollution seem obvious: I tell a story about a little girl, born two months too early, who is still in the hospital, whose lungs cannot handle any particulate, but that's all that seems to inhabit the air any more.

•••••••••••

You refer to the atmosphere as a "global commons" in need of management.

Tim Flannery: The way I've seen humanity handle commons best is at the small-scale, village level as in New Guinea, where I have spent much of my life working. Politics take a lot of time and energy to engage, but they aren't something we should be delegating to special representatives, or misrepresentatives. We need to develop a system where ordinary citizens play a more active role. We need to take turns governing ourselves, somehow, by creating a system in which we all get to engage at a deeper level, a system in which ordinary citizens are rewarded for self-governance. Governance is the one thing we should never give over to others. It's the one thing that as human beings we need to always be deeply involved in.

One way of doing this might be to have citizen juries deciding on budget items—after all, we're the taxpayers. That kind of involvement is clearly not the case in our current democracy; lots of hands intervene in the will of the people. But that sort of democracy is much more meaningful and robust in fending off dictators. It's partial democracies where dictators are strong, and you can see this today through global alliances such as those of Russia and the US, which are clearly getting closer—one a democracy and the other a dictatorship. At one level you can see they are not as far apart as many of us imagine.

•••••••••••

You spent time as a child living in Uruguay and Argentina under dictatorships. How did those political situations affect you?

David Rutschman: I was born in Uruguay in 1974, and we moved to Argentina when I was a baby. We left Latin America for the US when I was five, so I can't consciously access that time in my life very clearly, but it's there—in the body, the marrow, in the family stories of dear friends jailed and tortured. I think the concerns in my stories—terror and wonder, patterns of loyalty and betrayal, dreams and nightmares, sudden life-changing shifts—all make a lot of sense against a backdrop of life under violent military rule.

It might be relevant, too, that I didn't speak a word of English until we moved. I went from one language to another as a kid, and since language is part of how we create and interpret our world, I had an early, important experience of shifting from one world into another.

•••••••••••

In *Zoologies* you describe armadillos the size of cars that once inhabited the Americas. Picturing these *Glyptodon* shifts the scale of the landscape we tend to imagine. Was one of your goals for the book to alter the way people look at the world?

Alison Hawthorne Deming: Indeed, of course. Paul Martin, author of *Twilight of the Mammoths*, whom I had the privilege to interview when I was working on the book, opened my eyes to the amazing bounty of megafauna (giant elephants, sloths, bears, camels, shrub oxen) that existed in the Americas before the incursion of early human hunters. He thought we had something on our continent to match the pyramids in Egypt—dozens of gigantic creatures, like the *Glyptodon* that once roamed the very land we now inhabit. We know about dinosaurs. Why don't we know about these others? Martin thought "we were selling out our heritage" by not educating ourselves and our children about them—and their rapid decline after the arrival of human hunters. The story of human violence against animals is a long and deep one. If we hope to rewrite that story, we'd better understand it.

....

While conducting research for your latest book, you were stung by a bullet ant, purported to have the insect world's most painful sting. You describe the pain as "a strike on a bell cast from the purest bronze: clear, metallic, single-toned," calling it your "initiation into one reality of the forest." How did this encounter inform other realities of the forest?

David Haskell: The part where I was in the Amazon forest is more diverse than any other known place on Earth. Conflict and competition are therefore intense: weaponry and poison abound. The ant bite was one manifestation of this reality, a very tangible expression of the forest's life. But life in this forest is not all about conflict. Paradoxically, intensity of competition, predation, and parasitism in the Amazon has caused evolution to forge unions among allies. So instead of separating life into "individuals," the forest has instead welded networks. These networks take many forms: roots melded with fungi, ants working with microbes, animals uniting in groups. The ant bite underscored the intensity of conflict but also pointed toward other realities, processes of cooperation.

•••••••••••

Scientists have recently revealed the influence of ancient Native Americans' controlled burns of forests and grasslands. What do you know about this research?

Philanese Slaughter: I love reading academic journals. I minored in Botany in college, so I was interested to see this evidence of Native Americans' impact on the landscape. My grandfather and great-grandfather both used controlled burns as part of their stewardship of the land. I should explain that the Native mindset toward land ownership is quite different. The Eastern Indians in particular did not think of the land as belonging to people, but to God. Human beings were also not considered the apex predator of the natural world but as brothers and sisters of all living creatures. In fact, the concept that land could be divided, owned by only a few men, and passed from one to another, underlies the whole patriarchal mess.

If you read much history, you'll find that when the "discovering" pilgrims came to this country, they described it as parklike. Well, there's only one way to maintain parklike conditions around wooded areas, and that's to burn the brush periodically, which the Cherokees did in Missouri, in Virginia, North Carolina, Tennessee. Clearing the litter kept the snake and tick populations down, as well as poison ivy, buckbrush, and other undergrowth.

I've participated in controlled burns, too. In the 1980s, several of us members of the White River band of the Chickamauga Cherokee took a state training course and staged a burn to restore balance on tribal land that had gotten overrun with succession plants. There are fire biomes. People have to understand that.

....

How do you hope your writing informs current events or scientific discoveries?

Kimiko Hahn: I enjoy writing on a range of subject matter, and in the case of the natural world I hope to draw attention to the outer real world, even though I dovetail into the personal. For those not interested in science, poems may be an offbeat way of learning about, say, extinction. For others, like myself, the sciences are intrinsically captivating, and a kind of portal into other themes and issues . . . but how would my poems inform events? By bringing artists (the "cultural intelligentsia") and artwork into the conversation.

••••••••••

You co-authored *The Insect Cookbook*, the preface of which suggests that eating insects connects us to "the entire ecological cycle of life on earth." How so?

Marcel Dicke: My motto is "There is no life on Earth without insects." When we're eating insects, we're engaging in so much more than just bringing in some energy. We have to think about what we're eating and why we're eating it. It's important to consider how and why we are producing our food. A third of all agricultural production depends on insect pollination. Without this, we would not have tomatoes, oranges, apples, strawberries; it would be a very barren world. Insects were here before the dinosaurs, and they survived the events that wiped out dinosaurs. They are still with us, and if we would be so foolish as to destroy ourselves on this planet, insects would not be destroyed with us—so, they give us broader ecological perspective. We are guests here as well, and we are not the dominant species on this planet, although in some senses it seems like we are.

••••••••••

How important is meat consumption to the global climate conversation?

Marcel Dicke: It's tremendously important. Eighteen percent of all greenhouse gases emitted come from livestock production. Calculations predict that if we were to reduce meat consumption, it would be a major contributor to a reduction in climate change.

Also, if you depend on one or two protein sources and there is a major shock, everyone will be affected. Whereas if you diversify your sources, you redistribute the risk. This answer is easy to give, but these shocks often come with warning signs we ignore until the real shock comes. In the meat-production sector at the moment you can see major changes. We can talk about China becoming richer and see that they're eating more meat. We should consider what that implies in terms of food requirements internationally, even though we don't see anything yet. In grocery stores in America and Europe no one has any idea that there's a food shortage, but if you look at the macro level you can see that things are changing. We can wait for a disaster to happen, but we can also move toward options that might alleviate a major shock or prevent it. Time is short, though, so we need to act now.

....

A man introduced a talk that you attended by pointing out that in New England the term *servant* is often used in lieu of the word *slave*, "because people don't want to remember the dehumanization." Although the issues of slavery and climate change are very different, the reluctance to be implicated in wrongdoing seems similar. Is there anything your examination of the language and narratives of slavery has revealed to you that could be applied in other instances requiring collective responsibility?

Wendy S. Walters: I've been thinking a lot about how often the words *migrant* or *immigrant* now signify people seeking refuge from climate-related conflict. On the local level, I think about the word *zone*. I do not live in a flood zone, but I am adjacent to one. I do live in an asthma zone in Harlem. This has been known for over fifteen years, and yet, still there has been little effort to mitigate the impact of the bus depot that is considered to be a source of the neighborhood's poor air quality. I wonder, what other zones am I subject to? Because I am busy with life, I don't do enough to understand how these maps of survivability are being drawn around my community.

....

In another interview, you say, "Fact and fiction can both serve those in power and those who are not." How have you seen fact and fiction best employed?

Wendy S. Walters: Many years ago, I read a story called *Bashai Tudu* by Mahasweta Devi. I read the translation from Bengali by Gayatri Spivak. In this story, which takes place during an agrarian revolution, a single man—Bashai Tudu—emerges as a revolutionary figure. There is a gesture he does, something like wringing the air with his hands, before he is killed. But then in another part of the country, another man is killed, and before he dies, he too wrings the air with his hands. This is a crude summary of a more important story, but I was impressed by the idea that one might through gesture align one's own identity with the ancestors who gave their lives serving those who might live in the future. To me, this is a way that fact and fiction are present at once, and it is incredibly powerful.

Retelling the same stories can undermine our collective opportunity to access power. People like myths because they know how they end, people like pundits because they claim to know where all the chaos is headed. But we are going to go where our stories go—the ones we dig up and the ones we invent. If we don't make better stories, the worst of stories will make us.

•••••••••••

What was it like to grow up Native in America?

Philanese Slaughter: Becoming aware of my heritage didn't really happen until we moved to the States in my teens. Because my father was in the military, I was born in Sacramento, California, and spent my first Christmas in Hawaii, on our way to Guam. I often felt like an outsider wherever we lived. But if you had said *Indian* to me, I would have pictured the little girl from India that I ran around with in the British school I attended while we lived in a suburb of London.

The culture I received came entirely through the lessons my

Grandpa Tommy gave me—and my brother, born nine years later. My mother's father was three-quarters Cherokee, as was his wife. They were both born in Missouri just after the Civil War. Grandpa lived with us for long stretches of time. That's something you'll find with traditional Cherokees and matrilineal societies. If my mother had had brothers, they would have lived with us and taught us kids. Or my grandmother would have, but she had had a stroke and was bedridden from the time my mother was five (the treatment at the time), so that role fell to my grandpa. He taught me how to smell snakes. The venom in poisonous ones gives them distinctive odors he taught me to recognize.

My grandmother's family had lived in the Ozarks of Missouri—on the side of a mountain where if you fell off, you'd land in Arkansas—since the late 1700s, when Dragging Canoe's people split up on the Chickamauga, so we were there before the removes. My great-grandmother's brothers and sisters went to Tahlequah with the Trail of Tears, but my grandfather avoided reservations like the plague. He didn't want to be on The Res after what Andrew Jackson had done. Andrew Jackson was a dirty word at our house. Grandpa would not even carry a twenty-dollar bill. If one passed through my friend Randy's hands—a Red Stick Creek Indian blacksmith who used to vend at local powwows—he would take the tip of his cigar and burn holes through Jackson's eyes, pop, pop! He was very good at it, very precise.

Indian Residential Schools still existed until the 1970s with their mission to "kill the Indian, save the child." They separated children from their parents, so they wouldn't learn their heritage.

They took their language and culture, cut their hair, alienated them from what the old folks were doing, and then sent them back to The Res. The reservation was a eugenics model that Hitler learned from and used to design concentration camps. Jackson was Hitler's hero.

Indians were subject to the Jim Crow laws. Until 1970-something, it was illegal to be Indian in Missouri. Indians couldn't own property. You couldn't sell a bag of beans. So Cherokee was not spoken at home, because children speak what they know. If it becomes illegal to exist where your family has lived for centuries, you go underground; you try to keep under the radar. We covered up our skin, so we wouldn't get dark.

···········

Your fragmented essay "I Thought You Were in Afghanistan" illustrates that a landscape torn apart by war cannot be processed according to standard conventions. Will you speak to how you determined the form for it?

Brandon Lingle: I collected a series of seemingly unrelated bits of information from my time in Iraq. As I reviewed my notebooks, I found many scraps that struck me, and I wanted to share them, but individually they couldn't sustain a narrative, so I tried to construct them in a way that does. I tried to include the fragments that weren't reported by the media or those that offer context to the stories that did make it into the mainstream. Michael Herr's

Dispatches, especially the chapter "Illumination Rounds," heavily influenced my essay. In that chapter, Herr collects a series of seemingly unrelated vignettes from his time in Vietnam. He leaves it up to the reader to interpret how these terrifying fragments form a larger narrative.

••••••••••••

As someone who serves both the military and the reading public, you likely have a different relationship than most to the idea of a "whole story."

Brandon Lingle: While the idea of the "whole story" is compelling, it's unattainable when one considers the fact that roughly 2.5 million Americans, plus thousands of coalition forces from forty-nine other countries, have fought in Iraq and Afghanistan. And those are just the numbers for those who participated on one side of the war. There are also the millions of family members, and other loved ones, who are forever changed, nor can we forget the millions of Iraqis and Afghans who have been affected. The world will never hear the vast majority of these voices, all of whom deserve to be heard.

I'm not sure it's possible for any writer to capture the "whole story." My position is further complicated as a military public affairs officer, because, for the most part, the military reports information to the media, whereas I try to take the material a step further—to interrogate and offer perspectives on the larger implications.

My mentor, Donald Anderson, writes in *When War Becomes Personal*, "If it seems to fall to the historian to make distinctions among wars and each war's larger means and ends, the trajectory for the artist, regardless of culture or time, seems to fall toward an individual's disillusionment, the means and ends of war played out in the personal."

....

What is the function of aesthetic violence?

Shane McCrae: I think that varies from artist to artist, and from piece to piece. With the poems I'm writing on Margaret Garner— she was a woman who lived as a slave in the decades before the Civil War, who tried to escape slavery with her husband and children, and who, when her owner caught up with her, killed one of her daughters and tried to kill her other children to prevent them from being returned to slavery—I use violence in order to suggest the atmosphere of constant violence in which slaves lived their lives. To that end, I want the violence to distort the poems, particularly the parts of the poems that aren't themselves violent. Although, obviously, I can't know or approximate what it was like to live as a slave, I can hint at what it might have been like to see much of life through violence. What I hope for these poems is that they will work against the seemingly always resurgent romanticizing of the antebellum South, so for me, at least, for now, the function of aesthetic violence is political.

....

How do you manage and relate to the distortion of writing about Margaret Garner through the lens of over a century's worth of hindsight?

Shane McCrae: From the beginning, I've wanted to be as true to the bare, historical facts of Margaret Garner's story as I can, and I've actually gone through a lot of anxious internal back-and-forth every time I've had to invent in order to make the poems work. The big, documented facts, I won't change. But I know I can't get certain aspects of the story right. The best I can do is try to take that 20/20 hindsight into account, and I've found it helpful, in that regard, to read slave narratives—not the longer, famous narratives, but the shorter ones that were collected by the Federal Writers' Project in the 1930s. Some of these expressed perspectives on slavery that I find deeply disturbing—not because the narratives are full of horrors (although, of course, a lot of them are), but because these narratives express a nostalgia for slavery, and some even mourn its end. Even if that nostalgia is itself the consequence of distortions, the idea that such a nostalgia could be felt by former slaves is all the corrective I can handle. Still—I think being open to such disturbances is part of trying to be a writer.

....

Have you ever known someone positioned as an agent of circumstances so marked that a single decision made amid them was character-defining?

Thomas Gibbs: This story comes to mind. "Imelda" is an essay by retired surgeon writer Richard Selzer. Selzer was a medical student when he was asked by the Chief of Plastic Surgery at the Albany Medical College, Dr. Hugh Franciscus, to be a translator on a medical mission to Comayagua, in the highlands of Honduras.

Selzer assisted with before-and-after photography of the patients needing plastic surgery for horrendous facial cancers and hideous congenital malformations of the face and mouth. Imelda was a fourteen-year-old girl who held a pink rag to her face covering her enormous defect. Her resistance to revealing her defect intensified her disfigurement. Selzer took photographs; Franciscus marked her for the surgery.

When the surgery begins Imelda suffers malignant hyperthermia. There is no ice, no means of reversing her temperature; she dies. The two doctors go out to the mother. The chief, Dr. Franciscus, tells the mother her child is dead. The mother holds his hand and tells him at least Imelda is going to God as a beautiful young girl. She does not understand that the surgery was not done. The mother says she needs to find someone to help her with the body and promises to return the next day.

When she comes back the following morning, she uncovers the girl and weeps at her beauty. Selzer looks down and sees the surgery has been done. Fine sutures correct her features. The medical student realizes that the surgeon had gone down to the morgue in the night, operated on the dead body, and corrected the anomaly.

I am guessing that Selzer went to medical school in the late fifties. Culturally at this time, fixing outliers was the mission. Normalcy was the standard.

Imelda's story shocked me because I don't know that I would have operated on a deceased patient, but the complex character of the plastic surgeon makes the narrative. The surgeon, an authoritative, arrogant, brilliant, too-superior-to-have-friends reader of medical books only, is broken by this case. It may seem the surgery was done to support the mother, but in fact the surgeon could not deal with this patient dying and his failure to fix the defect. He never goes on another mission; his surgery schedule is reduced, and he retires, not honored by this circumstance-directed response, but decimated by it.

....

Does your subject matter make it hard for you to write?

Brandon Lingle: As my life becomes more intertwined with conflict, I've become more aware of how war encroaches at home. It's insidious. And writing about war offers another avenue for such intrusions. It's jarring to write about tourniquets and amputations one minute and then help my children with their homework the next. Much of my work, so far, deals with trauma and human suffering, and sometimes it's hard to find hope. And that's a sad truth, despite claims otherwise: there is little hope in violence.

•••••••••••

In *Regarding the Pain of Others*, Susan Sontag writes that people thought for a long time the outrageousness of war would be clear if the horror could be made vivid to those far from it, but even acknowledging its madness did not end it. I realize I'm asking a difficult and perhaps unanswerable question, but what is a reader or viewer to do with the horror—and banality—of war that you evidence in your writing?

Brandon Lingle: Many of us will have to deal with trying to make sense of Iraq and Afghanistan for the rest of our lives. The effects will echo through our children and maybe even their children. Colonel Thomas McGuire, a professor and my colleague at the Air Force Academy, once said that it takes a nation two genera-tions of people to heal from war. In many ways our country is still dealing with Vietnam, Korea, World War II, and perhaps even World War I. There's not much one can do with the absurdity of war except, as Tim O'Brien wrote, "If there's a moral at all, it's like the thread that makes the cloth. You can't tease it out. You can't extract the meaning without unraveling the deeper meaning. And in the end, really, there's nothing much to say about a true war story, except maybe 'Oh.'" My essays offer just fragments from a vast ordeal and acknowledge the difficulty in understanding one's experiences.

....

You say, "empathy requires us to dig way down into the murk, deeper than our own feelings go, to a place where the boundaries between our experience and everyone else's no longer exist." This statement is so direct its profundity might go overlooked, for it positions empathy deeper than personal feelings. Will you elaborate on how you access its depths?

Wendy S. Walters: There are people who talk about empathy as if it's an intellectual exercise, often a flawed one, and there are those who experience it as pure feeling, frequently inchoate. My experience is more akin to the latter. I thought everyone was like that. Once I was driving with a teacher I admired and she said to me, "It's so hard to feel things for other people," and I responded, "I think it's so hard not to feel for other people." She looked at me strangely, shook her head. Later that evening, I went to thank her for inviting me and she said, "Oh Wendy, you almost fit in this time." Her words were devastating at the time. She thought I wanted affirmation (which she wasn't going to give), and I wanted company. That was when I realized I lived in a place she had no interest in getting to.

Now I understand better that people access the world in different ways. And while I try not to judge other people's explanations of how they relate to feelings outside of their own experience, I am pretty confident in how I process sensational input. It's messy, by the way.

....

I have witnessed my own and loved ones' abilities to feel for others grow as a result of personal grief, pain, and loss. Has the way you process sensational input changed over the years, or been changed by a particular experience?

Wendy S. Walters: Some of this came to light when I was in my twenties and living in Washington, DC. Often, I would walk home from the business/restaurant district along a main thoroughfare alone at night. On several occasions, taxi drivers followed me honking their horns and yelling I was not safe, that I should get in their cab. I did not trust the cab drivers any more than I trusted the men on the street, so I kept walking, sometimes running to keep myself feeling free. I was in DC, in some ways, to escape from grad school in Ithaca where I had encountered too many men who were certain I owed them more attention than I was interested in giving. One of them belittled me frequently in front of my peers. A married colleague sent me harassing notes and obnoxious mixtapes anonymously until he confessed, distressed and in need of comfort for his transgression. Another sad man would knock on my door in the middle of the night when he needed emotional comfort from some troubling encounter elsewhere.

As this was going on, I was just trying to come into my own mind, to gain perspective on what it feels like to hold authority. So it is not so much loss that has shaped my experience, but, rather, the frequency with which other people have tried to impede my space to feel what I feel, to know what I know.

III.

Sound Travels Through and Around Barriers

EVERY SPRING THROUGHOUT my girlhood, insects known colloquially as news bees emerged with the pollen and hovered nearby as if to tell you something, wings buzzing like radios broadcast from another room. I tried to make out their messages, as I strained to hear the muffled words of my parents talking in their bedroom after they kissed me goodnight. It was easy to imagine a hoverfly's presence companionable. They couldn't sting you any more than a ladybug who climbed gamely aboard an extended finger.

Because my grandparents' farm was surrounded by Jefferson National Forest, I grew up in a landscape that dwarfed its inhabitants. We lived under skies whose bright planets I pictured in geometry class when we learned about parallel lines that never meet. When lightning bugs filled the trees on summer nights, they warmed the reaches of space, gilded the darkness, stars come down to close the distance between us and the next galaxy.

The land was densely populated, just not by people. Deer roamed the woods and skies, along with foxes, eagles, possums, coyotes, snakes, field mice, mourning doves, and the ghosts of Cherokee and Tutelo tribes who had been killed or driven from their homes by settlers whose whitewashed version of history I inherited. Had the news bees I thought friendly in fact been reporting, they would have implicated me in past and present crimes. But the only communication they hoped to share was that the patch of goldenrod or violets I plucked was their territory.

As a child I felt I belonged to the natural world. I was of it, among the mating calls of tree frogs, crickets, and katydids that thickened the screens we opened on summer nights. Congresses of geese honked into alignment, just as my younger brother and I shouted from the backyard to find each other. Bulls bellowed their dominion behind plank wooden fences, while we fought over toys—until periodical cicadas scattered shot into rounds that silenced all of us. Thunder cracked over limestone bluffs that exposed geographical strata as textured as these sonic layers, which would have crashed into cacophony if not for the prolonged rest notes held by the mountains. Even as a child I knew this score unfolded not in 4/4 time but in 1/1.2 billion. I could hear only a minute fraction of the whole composition, but it encouraged me to keep listening.

Have you had any memorable encounters with a particular insect?

Kimiko Hahn: My sister and I had bunk beds, and being the older one I was on the top. I had a small window and for several mornings one week I noticed tiny pyramids of sawdust. I thought fairies must have left them, even though I pretty much knew that fairies didn't exist. When I finally told my parents, my dad was furious that we had *termites*. I guess I was eight.

•••••••••••

Your biography describes you as a radical faerie. What does that descriptor mean to you?

Sugar le Fae: Whew, that's a dissertation question. I was first introduced to the faeries in 2006, visiting a faerie sanctuary with my best friend in the backwoods of Tennessee. But I've met fae all over the world, and what it means to be a radical faerie probably includes anything you might imagine. Many faeries live in queer, intentional communities. Some urban, many rural. Faeries generally have a reverence for the Earth, animals, and each other. Sexual liberation. Many definitions of faeries include concepts such as radical love and radical self-acceptance. Faeries self-identify.

Anyone can be a faerie. I've met faeries of every shade, gender, and persuasion. Many are loudly outrageous. A good many are quite shy. We run the gamut of any international community, I suppose. My onetime roommate in New Orleans was the first straight male to be crowned a Faerie Empress, so there's room for everyone.

·····‥···‥··

Your name also contains the root of the word *faerie*. What do faeries signify for you personally?

Sugar le Fae: Sugar le Fae is my faerie name, and my pen name. Funny backstory: A decade ago, I was on a study abroad in Greece, and the teacher told us that *Zachary*, my given name, means *sugar* in Greek (*saccharine* and *Zachary* are cognates). Soon, all of my peers affectionately started calling me Sugar, and the name stuck. Years later, after I had been teaching college English in Nashville for a few semesters, students began to find me on social media. I decided to change my online presence to Sugar; however, some platforms require a last name, so on a whim, I typed Sugar le Fae, after Morgan le Fay, one of my favorite mythical figures. Like many rad fae, I connect with the amorphous spirits of the forest, whose ways seem mystifying and chaotic to muggles, and I've found the old adage to be true: Once you eat with faeries, you never return.

I recognized early the power of having a queer name. Other people's reaction, when I introduce myself as Sugar, speaks volumes about them, and that's another great example of faerie magic—I use the term in a few ways. Some people say providence or serendipity; I say faerie magic. I'm an atheist, agnostic, (culturally) Christian, who touts bullshit about astronomy. I like the idea that somewhere on the edges of perception, there are faeries conspiring to trip us up, sometimes for our own good, sometimes to wake us up.

•••••••••••

My favorite descriptions in *The Songs of Trees* are your translations of birdsongs, such as the pileated woodpecker as an "old man in no hurry to nail loose boards." Will you provide a sonic translation of the giant green ash that falls while you are listening to the forest?

David Haskell: The ash is a mountain stream slowed a thousandfold. We hear two melodies, both lively, yet moving in opposite directions. The first sound is of water's ensnarement by gravity, each splash the sound of descent, of the relentless rule of physical law. The second sound is of fish swimming upstream, life resisting the dead hand of physics: swish and slap of fish powered by the lust to breed. The fallen ash is animated by this tension between decay and new life, entropy and new order.

•••••••••••

Your series of paintings titled *Shed and Chandelier* depict unpeopled landscapes where broken-down sheds are hung with chandeliers. What inspired these images?

Sheep Jones: Driving the back roads of Maine, I see so many different dilapidated structures that feed my imagination. Some look lived in, some look like crime scenes, others as sites of rendezvous. Some are strange, some the animals have taken over. Most are abandoned, but the mystery of past habitation is what I think about when forming the openings and closings, the entries and exits, of various windows and doors.

••••••••••••

When did you start painting?

Marc Gaba: I started to paint seriously in graduate school in Denver, because there was a large wall in my apartment that needed a large piece of art. I could not afford a large piece of art, so I had to make one, and I didn't want something cheap, or something that was not art. I did paint earlier, but more as a hobby, something to do between writing poems in Iowa and earlier as an undergraduate in the Philippines. But I think it was in Denver, in the month before classes began, that I started to take it seriously, when the habits of thinking that I had developed in writing poems became transferable to the act of painting.

·····

What was growing up in the Philippines like?

Marc Gaba: Until my sophomore year in high school, I lived outside the capital in two places that had wide, open spaces—first in Tarlac and its sugarcane fields, and then later in Bulacan and its rice fields. There was a neighboring flying school where we lived in Bulacan, and part of its runway ran along the far edge of the lot. So I grew up with small planes flying above and around expanses of growing, green things, watching things like political upheavals on TV that ostensibly had nothing to do with what was around me. Of course, growing up in the Philippines also means typhoons, the Catholic church, American pop culture, and a silly cultural obsession with the "world-class." It's like being an element in a collage—which has made me believe that biography and identity couldn't ever have a causal relationship.

·····

I want to know more about how you think of identity, but first will you tell me more about that obsession with the "world-class"?

Marc Gaba: When something that a Filipino has done is astounding, many people here would say that the piece is "world-class." One respected art critic, for example, said that the abstract art that came out of here in the sixties is "world-class." It's like saying, "It's good work not only by local standards, but by world standards." I feel really embarrassed by that mode of praise, even though it did arise out of centuries of "colonial mentality," a habit of regard that makes anything foreign, or rather, anything European, intrinsically better. You could say that it's a reactionary response to the cultural insecurity or neurosis that it still really smacks of. It's also symptomatic of a disproportionate emphasis on the performative level of making art—as though creative work were more for show and less for the change it wants to make in the world, which becomes easier to miss when the attention goes to how something fares.

As for identity, I think of it as an assumption underneath and between selves, more like one of the operations in an equation, rather than one of the variables. It also makes me think of what Elizabeth Bishop has written, from "At the Fishhouses":

> It is like what we imagine knowledge to be:
> dark, salt, clear, moving, utterly free,
> drawn from the cold hard mouth
> of the world, derived from the rocky breasts
> forever, flowing and drawn, and since
> our knowledge is historical, flowing, and flown.

•••••••••••

Will you speak to how the ear, almost of its own accord, wends toward something?

Lia Purpura: Whatever lilt or lisp or accent that's apparent in my essays is likely born of the way poetry reckons with me. Sounds and shapes are in my ear—from an early life as an oboist (almost conservatory-bound) and an early focus on poetry, that highly concentrated way of working in small spaces. So the ear, indeed, reaches out, casts out past *idea*, creates a shadow space into which ideas shimmy.

••••••••••••

You have written that "One *thinks* with the ear." What trains the ear?

Rod Smith: Hearing a lot of poets read has been key, for me. I've been running reading series in one place or another every year since 1988 and have learned as much or more about poetry from that than from anything else. The differences are as interesting as the similarities, so one almost wants to question whether the following list should be considered to be writing in the same language: Charles Bernstein, John Cage, Robert Creeley, Kevin Davies, Heather Fuller, Allen Ginsberg, Peter Gizzi, Lyn Hejinian, Susan Howe, P. Inman, Lisa Jarnot, Anne Lauterbach, Alice Notley, George Oppen, Leslie Scalapino, John Wieners.

I'm also interested in the degree to which these differences manifest on the page. It's great to get the book and read along while someone's performing. It's a very quick way into the work.

So in the end I guess I'm saying that it's highly intuitive, but also a matter of, literally, information. The information one gleans from hearing others read, and then picks, either carefully or spontaneously, from all the available articulations what is right for one's own sensibility generally, as well as for the particular piece at hand.

•••••••••••

Since you express yourself in both poetry and film, how would you say each genre complements the other, and where does one pick up and the other leave off?

Raven Jackson: I don't think there's a clear boundary between poetry and film, and that's what's so exciting to me. I'm grateful I studied poetry before coming to filmmaking because, in my poems, I found my voice, my obsessions, the textures and worlds I'm interested in exploring. Likewise, I believe having a background in poetry gave me permission to explore structure and form in my filmmaking in a way I may not have allowed myself otherwise.

One true joy for me with film is working with actors. It adds another layer to what you aim to create. So many times, I've been on set believing I fully understand the moment I'm creating, and then it's in an actor's body and I'm seeing everything for the first time. There's nothing like that moment, that discovery: seeing something you've written, breathing.

One of my goals as an artist—and a Black woman filmmaker

and writer from Tennessee—is to put complicated Black girls and women onscreen. For example, in the current project I'm working on—a narrative feature film titled *all dirt roads taste of salt*— we follow Mackenzie, a Black woman better known as "Mack," through different experiences and ages in her life in Tennessee. In the process of writing the script, I've written more portraits of Mack than I will ultimately use in the film, but each unused portrait adds a layer of depth to her character and richens the world I've created for her to inhabit.

Creating complicated and layered Black women and girls in my work truly feels like listening. I approach each character like a real, breathing person and, if I listen, I can hear what they'd say or do in certain scenes and situations. There's often research, too, which works in tandem with simply sitting with the characters. People aren't just one thing. We contain multitudes. Contradictions. We don't always say what we mean. In the script, I'm currently fleshing out Mack's complicated relationship with her father. She loves him but also resents him. How does this dynamic manifest between them? What do the silences in their relationship say?

I'm drawn to create work that leans into the ways we communicate without dialogue. When I was younger, I remember watching my mother walk naked through the house. I've added a similar scene in my film. There's no dialogue between young Mack and her mother as Mack watches her move around the kitchen, sits with her. But there, in Mack's eyes, you see something spark and be seen for the first time.

··········

Your second poem in *Versed* references the "Issues of the Day." What issues cycle through your days?

Rae Armantrout: I was thinking of the "issues" constructed for us by the mass media, the ever-changing phrases we're presented with as a focus for our discomfort or fear, i.e. "the war on terror," the "financial meltdown," the "bail-out fatigue." They might as well be the names of faddish new dances. If paid performers (pundits) are thinking such "things" over for us, does that relieve us from the need to think or feel? Is that the purpose of such "coverage"? I suspect it is.

··········

Can we talk about what goes unsaid in your work?

Rebecca McClanahan: Probably, knowing the way I work, the unsaid is more of a musical choice, something to do with the timing of silence in a particular segment. But I do believe that the reader wants a job to do; a reader completes the transaction we writers set into motion. Readers—at least readers of literary texts—are very smart. They don't want to be told how to feel, or what to make of what a writer has already set in motion. Our job as writers is to compose the score and play our instrument as well as we can. The rest is the reader's job.

••·····•••··

In another interview, you say that you are "interested in that moment when reading begins," but it sounds as if the moment splinters instantly—since you consider it to dawn with publication. If that is the case, what would be the moment reading ends?

Tan Lin: Reading, as you seem to be referring to it, sounds like it originates somewhere and goes to somewhere "outside" itself— here, as you suggest, to a reader. But I prefer reading as part of a self-enclosed system, what I've called a reading environment, that manufactures its readers and where the readers are inside the system, as it were. By *book*, I mean something like the environment—communal, social, theatrical, anonymous—in which the book is processed, read through and in, distributed and redistributed in rooms, emails, or seminars, rather than the book itself. So I would say, given this, that reading doesn't end, that it is endlessly perpetuated, which is why books are read even when we don't read them, why we can know books perfectly well that we have not read at all, why skimming and skipping around in a book is just as adequate as a close (linear) reading. Reading is an ongoing process, and it's not ultimately very individuated or very unique to the person doing the reading. The moment is not split at all by either a book or its publication. Reading is just a bit of duration in the room in which a book is sitting.

••·····•••··

How does time enter art?

Marc Gaba: Let me frame my response first. As far as time is concerned, the tradition in art has focused on keeping it out, to create the timeless from which the power of art has been thought to spring; most of us have been trained to think of art as a defiance of time. One might think that time first entered into art as duration in film, the precursor of video art, but there, time is rhythm, with the artwork bearing time, so that time doesn't enter it and goes alongside it instead.

In my paintings that I call apertural, time does enter. Time becomes part of the painting's substance. The anterior panel's aperture lets in light, shadows the panel behind, so that what you see when you are looking at the painting includes the exact moment that you are looking at it. I don't believe this has been done before. Certainly, the occurrence of shadows is knowingly used in sculpture, but in sculpture it's done for aesthetic effects, and the shadows aren't present as shadows. One might also think that I'm riffing on Lucio Fontana's work but I'm not. According to Fontana, he slashed the surface of the canvas so that we might glimpse the infinite—which, looking at a Fontana painting, I don't think we ever really do, the way we do when we look at a Rothko. An apertural painting is an imaging of time, and not an image of *a* time, insofar as the painting has advanced all the moments in which it is seen. It's a space of time. *Without* being a fraction of time. I hope I'm making sense.

....

Because the aperture in these paintings of yours is fixed, unlike a camera shutter, it remains open, enfolding each view in shadows that layer time on the canvas, which we perceive, by degrees, as depth. Is that right? Because if so, I see this work in conversation with Picasso's cubist portraits, which do the opposite and flatten time by making concurrent multiple perspectives.

Marc Gaba: That's a beautiful paraphrase, but I think it's too soon to say that we perceive time as depth. It would be fairer to say that in this contemporary time when painting and its documentation are considered the same, my intervention and thought are saying, first, that you never really see a painting unless you are looking at the painting itself. Second, because I like to be ahead of myself (isn't that what education is for, anyway?) I'm also saying that even when you are looking at the apertural painting, you will remain incapable of saying that you have seen all of it. For as long as it exists, it will outlive human perception.

Apertural painting is definitely in conversation with Picasso, but only insofar as Francis Bacon is also present. Bacon already saw the falsehood that Picasso's cubism perpetrates, and so Bacon wins the good wine. Picasso is a genius recaster, the greatest colorist, greater than Bonnard, but Picasso's art has no truth. Whatsoever. When you begin to think about his formally, truly great portraits, the ones that are originally his, they say nothing. His achievement I think is in composition. But even in composition, his art is bereft of ideas. To be clear, however, I should say that a painting that is bereft of truth and ideas does *not* mean that it is bereft of art.

....

When your writing succeeds what does it manage to do?

David Rutschman: The writing I most admire shifts something in me as a reader, and I'd like to imagine being able to do something similar in the work I create. The shift can take various forms. Here are some: from familiar to strange, from tragic to ridiculous, from distant to near, from near to impossibly near.

The other way around works, too: from strange to familiar, ridiculous to tragic, etc. The shift is surprising, embodied. When I look back up from a page of writing that does this for me, the room has changed. It's alive in a different way.

Now, I don't know how often I'm able to make this happen for a reader. Probably pretty rarely. It's a high, high bar. And I'm open to readers having other kinds of experiences. But for me, at least, that's the goal I'm chasing. The big fish.

The goal that's beyond that goal, of course, is to create some sort of shift, and then use that as a baseline for another shift, and another one after that. That fish is even bigger, and even more rare.

....

Marc Gaba: How does revision figure into creation as you've described it?

Amy Wright: It may be the answer inside Blake's poem: A good revision frames art's fearful symmetry. When a line comes into its own truth, finally, I can't touch it, even if I change my mind about how it feels.

....

Marc Gaba: You say that you stop touching something once it has framed its own symmetry, but you still think about it, right? It is still a remnant of your thinking, but if it were still you, you would keep touching it. Once you feel that it has framed its symmetry, then it is already in relation to itself and not you.

Amy Wright: Insofar as possible, I want a work of art to become a vehicle through which everyone else can project their language.

Marc Gaba: Maybe that's why there is conversation at all and why we don't think of visual art anymore as something that can stand outside language. So much of contact is linguistic, so a piece of art can't even be understood without the talk about it anymore.

....

What inspired you to listen to trees like the cottonwood, ponderosa pine, redwood, and others?

David Haskell: Sound travels around and through barriers. It reveals stories and processes that are otherwise hidden. It is also an underutilized sense in botany, so tree sounds are both a rich source of stories and a relatively unexplored realm. I came to them mostly through meditation on soundscapes. As I teach students about birdsong, I invite the students into soundscape awareness exercises: small "laboratories" in attentive listening. As I deepened this practice, I came to hear the interesting voices in trees. These sounds reveal the form of trees: maple in summer and winter, pine in ice or wind, palm on a calm day and in a storm— amazingly different sounds. They also tell us about the lives of other species in trees, including the voices of humans whose lives are interwoven with them.

We're in a mass extinction, on a planet whose physical nature is changing so fast that human and nonhuman life are in crisis. We're also on a planet of great beauty, a beauty that emerges from the extraordinary stories of millions of species. We belong within those stories. This great collision of beauty and brokenness goes mostly unexplored, unremarked upon. Instead our culture turns the gaze inward, into our own species, as if we'd learned nothing of note about the world and its perils in the last one hundred years. How could we achieve this end? Perhaps first by defragmenting education, removing the illusion that one can study science without ethics, philosophy without ecology, art without evolution, business without biology. Then, listen to the voices of the world, not just the voices echoing within human culture. For example, we're deaf to trees. Is it then any wonder that in the first dozen years of this millennium the planet lost 2.3 million square kilometers of forest but regrew only 800,000? This appalling loss of forests ought to be of great concern to a species that depends on forests for air, water, and livelihood. Yet that species' culture is largely unaware and unconcerned. Our stories have yet to catch up to the realities that we live within.

....

You say, "I am as cynical as they come, and as believing." What keeps your willingness to believe alive?

Gerald Stern: Frankly, it is a bit of a mystery to me. I keep thinking, at this late age, that I am starting over again. I think I start over every morning. I talked endlessly about faith in a recent book called *A God in the House*, where a group of poets talk about this issue. I say a number of things there. Here is one sentence: "Poets—maybe all artists—get away from their own religious upbringing in order to *arrive* at a condition of faith." For me, faith and religion are not the same thing. I guess mine is connected with the prophets to a degree, issues of justice, but by showing affection, kindness, and love—if possible—and hatred of swords, in any form. For me, poetry is a way, though I may disguise it, a way of getting in touch with the *holy*, if that is the right word. I think the final goal is to find that what we call the sacred and the profane are not really separate. I sometimes have faith that that might happen.

•••••••• ••

What justifies your optimism?

Tim Flannery: Alfred Russel Wallace, a contemporary of Charles Darwin's, independently authored his own theory of evolution by natural selection the previous year, in 1858. What Wallace noticed was that although competition is the driving force of evolution, what it does in effect is build levels of cooperation so that guilds form, even within individual cells, to work together to gain an evolutionary advantage. That was a profound insight. And cooperation in fact is by far the more overwhelming aspect we see in the world today, although competition may get our attention when we see it on a wildlife show depicting a wolf and a coyote or something.

In the closing paragraphs of his book *Man's Place in the Universe*, Wallace speculates that maybe it is the destiny of humans to perfect the human spirit in the vastness of the universe. For me that is a promising endeavor.

IV.

Fast Friends

WHEN I MOVED into my first apartment in college, my roommate Manda began to school me in the ways of the world beyond the Blue Ridge. While my other roommates grew up in the mountains like me, Manda had grown up in a small city outside the capital of our home state, different enough from my hometown to show me that tendencies I thought of as my personality were a compilation of the culture I had been taught. First-year orientation had already taught me to clip my drawl and tighten my vowels. Lecture-hall chemistry had culled me from the future premeds. Tiki Barber, the University of Virginia running back who would go on to play ten seasons for the New York Giants and wrote poems about his wins and falls, had illustrated in our introductory poetry class that the muse loves what we love. But Manda defined my education.

Manda was the kind of brilliant that could wait tables until ten p.m., hang out with her floppy-haired boyfriend until midnight, finish an A-earning paper on *Middlemarch* by three a.m., and stroll out the door the next morning looking like a catalog model. First among us to partner at a law firm, purchase real estate, and double you over with laughter at her veneer-peeling assessments of acclaimed books and movies, she was also a siren with a Lauren Bacall gaze.

Once, she came to visit me in southwest Virginia. After a summer of our writing each other letters about books, lost loves,

Tori Amos, and Gustav Klimt, she wanted to see where I grew up. I tried to shock her by first leading her to a nearby ramshackle Victorian that had been abandoned after a neighbor's death, its shutters dangling like a haunted house's. She was gracious, though, and ready for anything; the real shock came when I showed her our actual house and she learned that our cat lived outside.

"Where does she go in the winter?" Manda asked, stroking Misty's blue-gray head. To this day, she mocks my answer. I knew our cat relished the outdoors and loved to hunt mice in surrounding fields, although we also fed her. More often than not, she slept at large, where she wanted, and out of sight. Sometimes when it snowed, she bedded in the pine-bark mulch landscaping around our house, so I told Manda she was probably drawn to its warmth.

"In the *shrubs*, where it's *warm*?!" she asked, appalled. Only Southern decorum kept her from turning us in to the nearest humane society.

Having grown up where barn cats fended for themselves and bolted whenever people approached, I knew cats might tame easily but at least some preferred to live wild. Ours seemed to have the best of both worlds, the other side of which Manda had not seen from the suburbs. I held firm on the ethics of outdoor pets, but her nerve caused me to question countless other assumptions, including the founding principle of nineties-Appalachian-teenage etiquette, which was not to say what you thought.

"Don't answer that," Manda said one afternoon after a knock sounded at our apartment door. It was a guy she was dating, and planned to see again, just not then. That was an option? It was as if she had just told me I could be a theoretical physicist *and* play banjo. Time and again, she claimed the kind of agency I was more accustomed to seeing in men: she argued her points in literature seminars, blew off local music stars and hockey players with a casual aside, and commandeered attention at the jazz club where college students were forbidden or ignored. She appropriated or surpassed the strategies of my grandfather, who pretended not to hear questions he did not want to answer; my father, who sold hundreds of insurance policies without seeming to try to sell anything; and my uncles, who inserted a wad of chewing tobacco, spat, and changed the subject. While my mother, aunts, girl cousins, and friends seemed more beholden to others, Manda, whose glance was honed fine as a samurai sword, showed me that a girl might try to please, but a woman did not have to be good.

Your first writing teacher, Bertha Harris, told you, "Literature is not made by good girls."

Dorothy Allison: The idea that great literature is written by nasty girls told me that nasty girls and women are my aunts. They don't act out of meanness purely for the sake of meanness; they give back what is given to them. When they're given respect, they return respect. When they're given contempt, they show you that the contempt is not justified. The wage of violence is violence, so I try to avoid violence, but confrontation I believe in. Holding people accountable I believe in, and that's nasty. It means telling the truth even when it costs you something, even when no one wants to hear it or talk about it. You have to honor your version of the truth and you have to really search for it and make characters that live up to that. A no-bones-about-it, we're-in-this-together approach is what I honor. My aunts were paragons of it. They were also self-destructive and fell in love with the wrong people and didn't necessarily protect their children, but they tried. I don't believe in simple.

•••`••••••

Have you ever communed with a specific animal?

Dinty W. Moore: An elephant. I was a zookeeper during my college years. Elephants are the most amazing creatures. I think they have minds that are every bit as complex as ours. And big, big souls.

••••••••••

You were a zookeeper! Will you share a story?

Dinty W. Moore: When I was twenty, at the height of my invisible male hormonal fog-spraying potential, a female gorilla developed a pretty strong crush on me. Samantha would just go nuts anytime I came into the main building where she was housed, even if I entered through a doorway at the other end of the building. She would bang on the bars, dance around, and jump up to look for me. Eventually the head zookeeper had to ban me from the primate wing entirely, because he was convinced that she wanted to pull me through the bars and, well, you know, spoon a little.

••••••••••

Why were you attracted to your first boyfriend?

Eileen G'Sell: It's hard to say who my first boyfriend was. The first boy I made out with was Ted Steiling (pronounced *styling*). I was attracted to Ted because he reminded me of Captain Planet—in physique, bone structure, and, most importantly, aqua-colored hair. We were at a ska show (mid-nineties) and pretending to be Muppet characters. I thought, "He should be my boyfriend." And soon he was.

But I also like to think my first boyfriend was Mark Schmidtkens, from the first grade. Mark and I sat next to this other boy, Gary Opitz, every single day on the bus ride to and from school. We were fast friends and played basketball during recess. I did not have a crush on Mark or Gary but was excited that I had real buddies who didn't say mean things about me behind my back, as had happened with the girls I tried (and failed) to befriend. Then, one day, inexplicably, Mark started teasing me on the bus. We were three to a seat, and I was always in the middle, Mark next to the window, and Gary by the aisle. So Mark says, "Why are you sitting so close to Gary? Is it because you *like* him?" I reply with something like, "I sit here every day, and I'm only close because 'three to a seat' is the school bus law!" His taunting continues and my indignation mounts. Gary just sat there; I had to do something. "Stop it!" I kept saying. He was like, "What you gonna do? What you gonna do?" then finally, "What you gonna do? You're just a girl!"

I snapped and socked Mark in the mouth. I can still remember how shocked (and pleased!) I was by this course of action. I was a shy kid and a perfect student. I never got in trouble. But here I was, hitting my best friend! "She's got you now, Marky!" Gary said. Mark's mouth was bleeding. I think he was in shock. I knelt (yes, knelt—remember, I was only about forty pounds here) in the tiny space in front of his seat and begged him not to tell our bus driver, a grizzled-out molester-looking dude who played his *Slippery When Wet* cassette every single afternoon. When Mark did NOT tell the bus driver, I found myself suddenly attracted to him.

•••••••••••

When in your life have you felt the freest?

Mateo Hoke: There's no one time I've felt the most free. The feelings of freedom I've experienced have come, I think, in moments in which I've pushed past fear.

Do you remember years ago I took you cliff diving? It was late in the season and the water level had dropped dramatically, meaning a higher jump into shallower water. I knew I should hike down, get in, and check the water before we jumped. I think we were both scared of what could happen if I didn't. But I jumped anyway. Forty feet at least. I still remember the image of my worn white shoes hitting the water, knowing in the next instant my life could be gone or unrecognizable. Drowned. Paralyzed. But that instant isn't burned into memory because of fear. It stays planted in my mind because for one nanosecond as my feet broke the surface I felt the full force of freedom.

•••••••••••

How would you describe your current relationship to fear?

Christina Mengert: If I were born with a giant leech on my back, I might assume that leech is part of my body. My imagination of the shape of my body would likely include that leech. When I looked at everyone around me, and saw that they also wore leeches, this would confirm my vision. My understanding would feel so complete that I wouldn't think to ask how it could be another way. This is how I understand fear, as a thing we accidentally assume to be intrinsic, but only because we have been wearing it for so long. More and more I want to watch fear as if it were an organism distinct from myself. It is important for me to relate to fear with distance, to study it as if it were an exotic turtle I could hold in my hand, turn over, and poke in the belly.

....

Your award-winning short film *Nettles* depicts "stinging moments in the lives of different girls and women," suggested by the reference in the title to the stinging plant. Will you give an example— from your life or the film—of memories that sting or stung, and explain how pain informs your work?

Raven Jackson: I was drawn to use stinging nettles as a metaphor for the film, because a sting is very different from a gash or deep wound. Most stings involve brief moments of pain. With *Nettles*, all of the chapters involve seemingly fleeting moments of pain in the lives of different girls and women. Yet, while writing the script, I tried to focus on experiences I felt the protagonists would return to, again and again, throughout their lives.

When I was younger—eleven or so—I always used the bathroom with the door open. I specifically remember sitting on the toilet in the bathroom the day my father, his head low in the doorway, told me: "You got to start closing the door, Ray." Looking at the closed door, I knew something about me had changed—or ended. It's such a small, specific moment, but I remember it as if I were still sitting there.

In *Nettles*, one chapter revolves around a fifteen-year-old girl who's approached by a man as she walks home on an empty road. The girl, startled, runs as the man yells: "I just wanted to talk to you." During the audition process, almost every single young girl I spoke to had had a similar experience. For the character in the film, it is the first time she is experientially made aware that safety isn't guaranteed. The moment is quick, and no physical contact between the two characters is ever made, but something significant has shifted. A weight has been awakened in her that wasn't there before.

Experiences, memories, and emotions that can't clearly be defined as one thing or another are deeply interesting to me and inform most of my work. Even in *Nettles*, yes, the focus is on stinging moments, but there are joys, flirtations, and beauty present in the film, too. I'm attracted to and strive to create work that is visceral, has an emotional stake for the audience, and speaks to the multitudes we all contain, the contradictions and fears.

....

Is there a particular work in which you invite "everything in," or at least more so than in others? If so, can you describe that process?

David Keplinger: I'd say I'm trying to do some of that in my new collection, *The Most Natural Thing*. It begins with an epigraph on Tantrism, which speaks of the whole universe as a body, of which the individual is only a part. The image of the body, its apparently separate parts working in and out of accord with each other but contained within the whole, becomes a metaphor for the entirety of existence. . . .

....

How do you think of the relationship between body and mind?

Sejal Shah: I think it's incredibly complex and also radically simple, made more complicated by addictive electronics and time spent in cars. You can lose the feel of the body on the earth, walking. Meditation, flowers, rituals. Eating good food. Getting enough sleep. Lately I feel I need to do something that connects me to my body again. I spend a lot of time on the computer. Since I left New York City and moved back to my hometown of Rochester, New York, I drive to most places. I miss walking to work, to the post office, to yoga class, to the grocery store—these things I did for years while living in Manhattan and Brooklyn. I don't miss most parts of living in a large city, but I miss a way of daily living that in its own way felt village-like, anchored in a neighborhood and walking, being around others.

....

There is a lot of walking in your collection *The Body Is a Little Gilded Cage*. Will you describe a memorable walk you have taken?

Kristina Marie Darling: One summer I was staying in an enormous old house in New England. I would make myself take long walks in the sunlight so as not to be overcome with melancholia. On one of these walks, I came across a painstakingly manicured garden. Behind the flowers were ruins of another garden, which had been abandoned years ago. I never asked anyone about it. It seemed like everyone who lived in the house took their walks there, but no one ever mentioned the ruined part of the garden.

....

"There is no devil as we've come to think," you write in *The Prayers of Others*. What is the devil, you think?

David Keplinger: When I wrote that line I was thinking about the one devil, the one image which was the embodiment of evil, chewing on Judas in the basement of hell, who comes to reign terror over the lives of the good and who comes to bear out punishment on the lives of the not-so-good. I was thinking of the devil on one shoulder and the angel on the other. In contrast to that is the image of Dionysus, one of chaos, drunkenness, comedy, change. The Greeks embraced unpredictability; they equally embraced the illusion of a separate self who served in the world, embodied in the image of Apollo. They saw no need to put these forces at odds, necessarily . . . yet I grew up Catholic; I have a little vestige of the Old World in my thinking, too.

·········· ··

Do you relate to sex in terms of freedom, desire, love, power, science, vulnerability, or something else?

Marc Gaba: Freedom, you bet. Desire, yes. Love, of course and of course not always, but self-love, self-affirmation, definitely. Power, no but forces, yes. Science, science is everywhere there is matter, a frightened mind, and care for fellowman. Vulnerability in the sense of risk, yes. I broke up with Number Two because the thing became a health risk; the bastard kept a secret life from me (among other unacceptable things). Vulnerability in the classic female sense of emotion, no. I recently read a part of *Bhagavad Gita*, and discovered via the copious notes that in Hinduism, sex can be a path to higher consciousness (hence the exemplary Indian tolerance of all sexuality). Which makes me think of how some saints felt Jesus as sexual excitation.

I relate to sex in terms of spirit. Maybe that's why, after sex with a hot Irishman years ago, he couldn't believe how good it was (because most gay Filipinos are bad in bed, in his experience and mine). He had to ask, "Where did you learn to have sex like that?" I said, "America," and he hated my response, and proceeded to attack—of all things!—the ubiquity of corn syrup in American food! So that's postcoital talk with a European for you. Anyway, when I say I relate to sex in terms of spirit, I don't mean to suggest that Catholic sinners are best in bed. Perhaps only if they truly understand Catholicism and experienced the maddening courage it took to touch another person's body for the first time, and can understand parts of the Bible as historical, or can read as great scholars do: in context. But even as I say that, there have been moments when homosexuality did feel evil. Something in the air—difficult to describe except as a marked difference—in the light—something hazy, warping vision, that it also made clear and intense. The word *trespass* comes to mind, a feeling that an other-worldly, bad spirit encroached. Or perhaps it's that there simply are diabolical people, gay or otherwise. They express their sexuality in utter bad faith, the "I love you" translating as "I commit to this evil" to the sharp-eared. What to do with that? To a younger person who might read this, do take care, we're all different.

···········

You say in your essay *"Hic Sunt Dracones"* that we need dragons because the "world, like the World Wide Web, has no end, no edge." Later, you specify that dragons represent boundaries "for us, who need limits if we're to know these worlds and our places in them." Will you give me an example of a dragon that has helped you to know or find your place in the world?

Eric LeMay: Perfection, especially that idea of artistic perfection, has become more and more menacing and dragon-like as I've grown as a writer and person. I began my career with a belief that the perfect artwork should not only be the aim of any serious artist, but also that it was redemptive, worth any measure of sacrifice. I think the belief came out of that desire we have when we're young to really do something, really achieve something. I still believe in the transporting power of art, but experience has taught me that you get there—at least I get there—by fucking up and around.

•••••••••••

Do you know anyone who's perfect at something?

Coleman Barks: My granddaughter Keller, age eleven, is a perfect point guard. She sees the whole court in front of her, all possibilities. Then she acts without thinking, like an animal, no prethought, no regret. Very beautiful.

•••••••••••

If you had to set fire to something, what would you burn?

Kristina Marie Darling: Selections from Freud's *Studies on Hysteria*.

·········· ··

You lived in a papermaking village in Japan in the late seventies. How did living there shape your aesthetic?

Sheep Jones: Living in Japan changed my visual vocabulary. Back in those days, my husband Charlie and I were drawn to Asian art, from the characters to the high-contrast ink drawings. Much of the symmetry that dominates my work, coupled with high contrast and a number of visual icons, stems from our stay in Japan. Look at bento boxes, tatami mats, rock gardens—all are visually contained by boundaries.

·········· ··

In your essay "Skin of the Earth" you lick your finger and taste your father's ashes. It is a startling image of communion. Will you talk about how you access intimacy as a writer, and how choice factors into experience?

Nicole Walker: It's one bonus to having fluid boundaries. I may not say *no* to you, but I also may never consider the appropriateness of eating ashes or biting someone on the ear while a Bonnie Tyler impersonator sings "Another Eclipse of the Heart," which I did at the drag club to my ex-boyfriend's ear. I just wanted him to turn around. Choice seems too high-minded a concept, but perhaps willingness to disregard good sense and to act by desperate syllogism—my dad is dead; I must keep him with me; therefore, I must eat him—is how you write best what you live.

....

Since the final chapter of your essay collection *Quench Your Thirst with Salt* echoes the title of Maurice Sendak's *Where the Wild Things Are*, I wonder if that children's classic is where your story as a reader begins?

Nicole Walker: That idea of being wild—of being boundaryless, of transporting the imagination from here to there—is what I love about writing. I also love the form that wilderness imposes on the wild. That hawks must eat baby squirrels. That bark beetles decimate drought-stricken pines. That Max must go home for dinner. The wilderness is beyond generous, like any good writer and good reader, but to be truly fair, there must be some habits, if not rules, imposed on expectation. Upsetting expectations is fun for the writer, but satisfying a reader is the true honor of writing well.

....

How has your relationship to sex changed since adolescence?

Marc Gaba: It probably follows the usual narrative. First it was about shame and fear, then it was about courage: that was adolescence. Then it was about style and self-respect, ego, habit, statistics—I feel like a frat boy saying that, but it also coincided with exploration that was as much experiential as social; I love that phase most, experiencing desire without care for class or reputation, no thought of mother and dad and catty relatives whatsoever. Then it was and is about pleasure, about which nothing is precious. At forty-one, I'm curious when its interest would die down. Can it, if pleasure? What will wisdom say, given a chance to speak to it? What has never changed throughout is the pleasure of a degree of secrecy, and that candor like this is its mask, something that only the trustworthy could say. I claim that you can trust me, and I wonder if you agree.

············

Amy Wright: I trust your candor. And I agree that candor can safeguard secrecy. I'd say we create the intimacy we crave by the degrees of our willingness to open to it. I have also remained interested in secrecy in relationships because I allow myself more freedom in my sexual fantasies than perhaps any other area of my life. Right now, because I'm in a romantic relationship with a partner I trust deeply, I have ventured into desires I don't yet recognize the roots of, as I have in the past recognized surrender as a way of disowning the desire I was taught to deny as a girl growing up in the South. But I should clarify that I am not interested in secrecy in terms of withholding from others but of bringing to light the depths of ourselves.

•••••••••••

Marc Gaba: Please go on—about "bringing to light the depths of ourselves."

Amy Wright: I wonder now if time enters these moments, as in your apertural paintings, although the light is internal. Attention illuminates them, but time might ignite them with the spark of change. My fantasies of surrender didn't fade so much as shift. After years of projecting desire onto others, at last I admitted it as mine. I recognized the shadows of desire's origins, but seeing didn't change them. If anything, I felt justified, even feminist, throughout my twenties by reclaiming desires I imagined boys could seize right away. What changed was the opposition. Picture a young woman in black thigh-highs looking over her shoulder into a full-length mirror, camera in hand: to be desirable the only aperture for her desire. I imagine you can see that surrender to such a dynamic was only playing at surrender. What I was after was the freedom to desire, or to lack resistance to it, which did lift, but only after I began to trust my desires to be good.

•••••••••••

When in your life have you felt the freest?

Marc Gaba: The image of fields on either side of me driving down a country road in Gerona comes to mind, but it's just the feeling of open space, not of freedom. You are right to suggest there are degrees to freedom, yet I've only ever felt *freer* rather than *freest*; I wanted to say simply that I am freer and freer by the second. If only there's a way to say so without implying that death is some kind of freedom, because it isn't.

•••••••••••

How do you recognize that movement? Are you becoming freer to or freer from something?

Marc Gaba: I recognize it as a freedom from the hegemonic tendencies of my parents (whose marriage was annulled). My mother, who doesn't support me, still wants me to get a regular job. And without saying so directly, my father, who doesn't support me either, thinks I should paint figurative, bullshit art. The older I get, the better I'm able to see them for what they are. Since I work as an artist, my bank statement is a classic example of fluctuation, and I confess that an interest in inheritance has always been part of how I imagined my future, an interest that's looked down upon by stupid moralists who can't see it for the basic pragmatism of it. Of course, that is the source of their power over me, and I've recognized the reliance in my imagination as the cage. The more different I am from family expectation, and the more relaxed I am about the difference, the freer I am.

In my darkest hour, when I had nothing to eat for about two weeks (who knew you could do things with flour and sugar and water!?), I learned to relax into the weird, severe poverty in the condo my mother gave me. I've faced the possibility of dying three times or so before, so I recognize the "movement toward freedom" as an affirmation of my unusual life and my increasing commitment to being an artist, even if it means having to go through the severe poverty again. It's not that I want to crawl about—I do want to build an architectural house for myself—but if severe poverty is what it takes to be myself, then it's the price I pay, and it will have to be okay.

V.

It's Always an Argument

ONE MORNING WHEN I was eight, I scavenged the field beside our house for a good chunk of sandstone to load into my backpack and arm myself against the Jackson boys. The wiry, dark-haired brothers were last to get off the school bus, after me. State maintenance on our gravel road ended at their stop. Since they lived deeper in the mountains, someone had to drop them off on weekday mornings and pick them up each afternoon beside the string of mailboxes where mail service ended, and then ford Cove Creek twice to get home. I couldn't see where they lived from our house—just the foot of the mountains where the dirt road wound out of sight—but I had seen their mobile home clinging to the wooded mountainside like a shelf mushroom, T-shirts and jeans flapping on the line, when Dad drove us past on his motorbike to show me the old logging road.

I didn't throw the rock or swing my pack against them, as I must have planned, but the ten pounds it added to my frame fortified me the day I carried it to school. I only carried it once. Mom dropped the bag in shock when she lifted it from my shoulder and made my plan laughable. She would have said something to the bus driver if she thought I was in danger, but she trusted that the boys were just teasing me. And they were, but I was determined to fend for myself. If I were older, maybe I would have used reason or believed I could use reason in such situations. As it was, conversation played no role in the social structures we were being taught.

Years later, I recognized in the Jackson boys what I found myself attracted to—the unknown, beyond the beyond, where a seeming wilderness of national forest began. I imagined their world to be defiant and free in a way mine might never be. For years we rode in and out on the same road together, but where we were going and what I wanted out there in the world beyond Mudlick Road had become suspect. Only art could compare to the other direction that road led, away from society and social obligations, deeper into the Blue Ridge. And if art could not be fed like a fallen tree to a fire, or plucked like raspberries growing wild on the mountainside, what was its draw?

In the *Critique of Judgment*, philosopher Immanuel Kant says, "Art is a mode of representation which is purposive for itself." By purposive he does not mean that art has a set purpose, like a stapler—or that art exists for art's sake, as Swiss philosopher Benjamin Constant first simplified the point—but that art, on reflection, has a purpose particular to it, which is necessarily indefinite. For instance, Amiri Baraka's poem "Wise I" might goad someone to express her "oom boom ba boom" when others would suppress it. Kiki Smith's porcelain sculpture *Woman with Owl* might illustrate a merger for one seeking kinship with nature. The possibilities for such purposes are endless, but if a work serves none, Kant likens it to chance rather than art.

In addition to these individual purposes, Kant continues, art has a common purpose, which is to advance a culture's power to communicate the processes of the mind. Various examples come to mind, but one that best illustrates this power in relation to the purposes of other common tools is Kell Black's *Ace Stapler, circa 1950*. Sculpted from manila file folders, this paper stapler would crumple if you attempted to fasten a document. Instead, as an object of contemplation, his life-sized model calls attention to its design and context. One notes the round lever as it rises to meet the palm, unlike the flat, rectangular tops of later models. The wide base has gravity, the top bulk, though in this form the stapler is almost weightless. The working mechanism is at rest, like an office admin at a water cooler. Like a paper miller on a smoke break. Like the mind between thoughts.

Black's stapler belongs to a series in progress that includes a number of utilitarian objects—all in a creamy monotone that displays them being as unaccustomed to labor as pale-skinned Victorians. Like mannequins, or Platonic ideals, they stand in for the apotheosis of stapler, clothespin, light plate, etc. You have interacted with these objects before, some daily, without deeming them worthy of study. Too common for magnificence, too familiar. Or they have slipped into another era, as with the pencil sharpener. They archive slippage. In some cases, their designs won over hundreds of patents, for economy of production rather than perfection of form. To look at them is to find our purposes at odds. To look at them is to know our purposes transcend the tasks at hand.

Aesthetic work is impractical. To coil a thread of paper that will never spring to pin a shirt is not pragmatic but it is not without purpose. Such creations break the chains of supply and demand, democratize beauty, and defy the capitalist paradigm, or can. Objects in reproduction differ by our relationships to them and dismiss that difference, as we have and have not, who hang sheets on the line, flick on the overheads when we get off work, and string lights from our porches. Removed from these purposes, paper tools serve another. As we do with periscopes, we peer through them over the obstructing ridges between us, which separate one life from another, one way of thinking from another.

Some of us think in numbers, others in lines, angles, time frames, etc., yet when we lift our hands to a light plate—rather than a dimmer knob or motion sensor—it snaps declaratively: the capital letter of an entrance, the period for an exit. Or it would, if wired. In paper, the snap hangs like a breath. We eye the switch, open palms by our sides.

When I asked Kell, who is also a friend, why he undertook to true the angle of a stapler that can never be fired, he said, "When you start looking closely at something, you see how everything is connected. You find biology, politics, gender, history, nature, and pop culture intertwined." He says the modern clothespin stands in for the rise and revolution of industrialism in America. But it isn't crucial to him if viewers recognize each object's historical context, which one of his reviewers has said makes his work "effortlessly informed." Kell holds up a clothespin and says, "Function is inherent in its form—as in one of Leonardo's anatomy drawings. We comprehend it at once because the human form is embedded in its lines."

He shows me half a dozen of the clothespin patents filed

between 1830 and 1880, but not popularized. Many of the designs would have solved the flaw of the iconic clothespin, which can twist mid-pinch and pop its spring. There are Quaker-like designs, wooden toggles in lieu of metal, springs that loop like signatures, bodies with joints like hieroglyphs. "The silhouette decides whether a piece has magnetism," Kell says. "The test for me is: Do I want to pick it up?"

But the test might also be whether a model can trick you into using it, as one of his paper folding chairs nearly did. He shows me this early piece, which was part of a string quartet in paper he exhibited in the early eighties. "I have to hang the chairs on the wall, rather than set them up," he says, demonstrating how the seat hinges and folds together. Once, after setting up one of the chairs for the exhibit, he carried in the violin, turned around—exhausted from being up half the night finishing this piece—and stopped himself only inches before sitting down. Even atop his dining room table, the chair has the gravity of a piece of furniture.

Or perhaps the test for these works is how people on the street respond. One afternoon, Kell boxed up some of his paper objects and showed them not at the usual galleries or museums, but curbside to a group of guys running a lawnmowing service. They ogled the pieces, exclaiming in wonder as they held and handled them. "What I hope to do," Kell says, "is call attention to the ordinary phenomena all around us. To help people see things in a different way."

He lifts *Ace Stapler, circa 1950* from the piano, and asks: "Do you see how it rises from its pedestal like the Sphinx?" His greyhound Gidget strides by. "Or a greyhound," he adds, "which is an Egyptian breed whose ancestors, scholars say, served as models for temple drawings."

"Geometry teachers love to have me come talk to local elementary school students," he continues. "Looking at these objects, kids can see how they're made, and it fires the imagination. But that's not why I make them. I make art for very personal reasons." When I ask what they are, he says: "There's a surprise when you fix the final part of a work. It's like listening to Bach: all of my molecules line up when every note is in its proper place."

Kell's musical reference is not casual, since before he went to art school, he trained as a harpsichordist at a Vienna conservatory. Of the influence of music on his art, he says: "There's a grammar to the fugue. The form dictates the rules. There are similar limitations to be abided when working in paper. It can be cut, folded, or glued; within those three constraints, what can you do?"

The many possibilities are illustrated in the books that helped define Kell's artistic reputation: *Paper Chess*, *Paper London*, and *Paper New York*, which include models of queens and pawns, Westminster Abbey, the Empire State Building, etc. But more than the iconic buildings and pieces, what snags my heart are the paper hot dog cart, the four paper pedestrian pop artists crossing Abbey Road, the invitation to readers to cut out their own knights and bishops and join in his fun.

He opens a folder containing paper doilies from which he has carved scenes from the history of flight. There is a zeppelin, a pusher plane, Apollo 11. The monumental aircrafts connect to their lace borders by paper strings as thin as a pin—as if to make apparent the fragility of even the grandest human achievements.

I wonder aloud if Kell doesn't worry about the durability of his work. He says: "At the conservatory, I spent a year learning to perform a piece that vanished into the air seconds after I finished playing. It's not the artifact that interests me but the art, and what the vernaculars of each art form can communicate."

I think about what the rock I loaded into my backpack would have communicated to the Jackson boys had it not remained hidden: Naivety, desperation, helplessness? Instead, our homes, clothes, parents' cars and jobs communicated for us.

Kell tells me that next he plans to make objects that have helped people see the world differently, beginning with microscopes and sextants. He shows me their forms in profile—the orbs and starry angles contained in their silhouettes—and I remember how the boys' faces shone in the sunlight when I looked at them askance.

As I turn to go, I notice that, although I didn't see when, Kell had removed the note he had taped to the door, which invited me to enter without knocking. It was a small touch, but one that allowed me to come into his home as he and his wife do, familiarly. Yet it was an act akin to the application of art to life, a gesture that could, when the eyes meet, prompt a conversation you might never have had.

What defines class?

Dorothy Allison: It's always an argument, because class is defined in opposition, and to some extent in denial. Especially in American society, there is a lot of shame and refusal. To a large extent we have the delusion that we are a classless nation, and that's just a frank outright lie.

The essential onus on the working class is to be always inappropriate and embattled. You're always in an argument with the over-class about who and what you are—particularly in the South but also in other regions. They have complicated gradations of class in California, yet we have very simple-minded ways we think about socioeconomics in this country. We think in terms of the broad categories of working class, middle class, upper class, but if you ask someone to define herself it always gets more nuanced.

My sisters, for instance, never wanted anyone to know that we were poor, so there was a refusal to discuss our position in the class structure. If someone did try to talk about it, my sister Barbara would say, "Well, we're really middle class." Our stepfather always had a job, our mama always worked, but the working poor is still a phenomenon—and I define the working poor as people who can't eat every night. I know it sounds trivial and petty, but the struggle was to go to school five days in a row without having to wear the same outfit three times. Kids are ruthless. They notice all those details. All of the earmarks of being raised poor were there, but we pretended with the rest of America that we were part of the great middle. It's very hard to change something you can't acknowledge.

....

Why distinguish between middle and working class when the top 10 percent of America's wealthiest families hold 85 percent of the nation's wealth?

Dorothy Allison: I often conflate the upper and middle class, although they aren't the same. It's just that we have almost no access to the upper class, so we really can't impact them in any immediately recognizable way, but we can impact the middle class—sometimes through literature.

I deeply believe that the best American literature is working-class literature, and part of it is the perspective of working-class escapees, and I use that term *escapees* advisedly. I don't think you genuinely leave your class of origin but, like the discovery that you're queer and a bit like the discovery that you're smart, it divides you; it separates you out.

Name the works of genius by American artists and you'll find that working-class artists created them because they had nothing to lose. The choice is life and death: you will either be murdered outside the Greyhound bus station in your hometown, or you will go to New York to become a dancer or a singer or a poet or writer of fiction. And you find that over and over again. When you find great artists and you query them you find out that they came from a small town, and they're estranged from their family. You know why. Even if they weren't queer, they're queer in that broader context of being unacceptable.

•••••••••••

What was it like to grow up Black and female at the beginning of the twenty-first century in Tennessee?

Raven Jackson: Growing up Black and as a Black woman, one of the most important lessons I've had to learn and relearn is how to take up space. I often return to James Baldwin's quote: "It took many years of vomiting up all the filth I'd been taught about myself, and half believed, before I was able to walk on the earth as though I had a right to be here." As a twenty-nine-year-old looking back on my younger self, I see how I often made myself small—would fall into the walls if I could.

One humid day in my preteens, my sister and I went to the corner store by our house in search of candy. When the cashier accused us of stealing, we stood there, quiet. Our hands still. Even now, in stores, I'm always aware of my hands and the employees likely looking for them. Earlier, I mentioned "stinging moments." What happened years ago, in that corner store, is one for me.

When I think of growing up in Tennessee, I also think of the smell of my great-grandmother Mary's house. My cousin TJ chasing me after I pushed him to his knees on a trampoline. My sister's face after I threw one of her Barbies high into a neighbor's tree. My Aunt Neicy introducing me to historical romance novels as birds screamed in the trees outside. Even though some of these moments happened in Alabama or Mississippi, when I think of my childhood, these moments float to the surface and hold out their hands to me.

··········

You've said, "One of the strengths I derive from my class background is that I am accustomed to contempt." How has contempt served you?

Dorothy Allison: Being despised is very hard to survive as a child, but once you don't die [laughter] you gain a kind of resilience. And it generates in you a reverse contempt that undercuts it. But it can go bad. It can go sour. Remember that all of the ways you derive strength can cut the other way. I've noticed that it happens about once a decade where all of a sudden they start using that language of contempt, and I have to stand up to it all over again with a whole new generation with another vocabulary.

For me it's complicated by the fact that they seem to coincide with periods where I'm struggling with my own spirituality. I couldn't quite go back to the Baptist church, but I go to Quaker meetings. I have deeply complicated feelings about the concept of God, but I genuinely cannot believe that we are merely meat and electrical synapses. I believe in the spirit, and that has been a place of struggle, which is also about class because people say, "You just think that because you were raised with Pentecostal music." Maybe, but you know gospel music won't kill you. It'll give you some places where you can derive strength that isn't about hating yourself.

•••••••••••

Given the biases inherent in any narrative, do you measure a story's truth by its range or consideration of perspectives, or by something else?

Wendy S. Walters: Many people expect philosophy to be the mechanism for finding truth, which is great if one loves philosophy. But philosophy is full of bias that does not suit my personhood. I get bored with arguments about the weight of one perspective over the other. Narrative can feel like truth because it leaves a trace in the imagination. I carry so many narratives long-distance without feeling burdened by the weight of them. And narratives exist in time, which for me is part of the reason they are compelling. But you are right, narrative isn't always about truth. Truth moves through narrative, it's in the music of the piece, how it resonates in the ear. There is truth in the shape of a work, too, how it looks. Truth is also subject to time—the moment it was made and the moment it is recognized—and because of that truth might not always hold steady as narrative.

·····•••·••

"Nothing should be unknown," you say in your poem "Eleven Minute Painting," which reminds me of Laura (Riding) Jackson's determination to reveal the truth in her writings. How do you relate to her ideas?

Tan Lin: I have read the first couple of pages of nearly everything by her, especially her prefaces, which she revises like a blackboard. I like the blackboard effect vs. the truth quotient in her work. I like the fact that all statements of the truth have to be surrounded, as with a blackboard, by statements of truth value. Meaning is always assigned by a party who is interested.

·····•••·••

What was your first job?

David Baker: I started teaching guitar at age thirteen. Next job: playing solo or with musical groups and bands at around fourteen or fifteen. I had a steady band for weddings, school dances, Elks clubs and such, and then I started playing in the lounge of the local Ramada Inn on Wednesdays and a local Italian restaurant on Saturdays at fifteen. All during this time I was mowing yards, too, up to ten or so in the summers. Regular yards were $2.00 and big ones were $2.50. I still love to work in the yard, in the trees and grass and bushes and gardens and flowers and back in the deep woods.

···········

In *Working*, Studs Terkel connects workers across class and income brackets. Is it still possible in the twenty-first century to find commonality in work?

Dorothy Allison: It is possible. What Studs is talking about is valuing the work, valuing the society that is shaped by the work they do. He didn't equate the qualities of a CEO with a guy who digs in the mines, but he did equate the commitment to a shared society in which work is valued. He was a huge advocate for that. He was really talking about community in everything he did, which is why I loved the man. We shared the hope for a just society. In a just society we would all be valued equally for the nature of our contributions, even though our contributions vary widely.

···········

How did you and Terkel know each other?

Dorothy Allison: We knew each other from the American Booksellers Association (ABA) meetings. We were both speakers in, was it 1992? It was a huge weekend, because it was him, Hillary Clinton, Colin Powell, and that idiot who wrote the Chicken Soup books. We all wound up in a green room together. Hillary Clinton was in another room with Secret Service agents until shortly before we went onstage, but I got to meet her. (She had multicolored eyebrows!)

I loved Studs Terkel's books, and when I love books, I remember them, so when I met him, I quoted some lines from one. He laughed and grabbed my arm and shook me and boomed, "I knew I liked you!"

•••••••••••

You mention in *Neck Deep and Other Predicaments* that Michael Martone sends you periodic postcards. What does your friendship with him mean to you?

Ander Monson: For Martone, I'm not sure what attracts him to postcards or why he keeps sending them to me (and to a whole bunch of others, I expect). It's the compression, probably, and the byzantine quality of the mail service. (General delivery, for instance, is a favorite nook of his—that old technology.) I've only sent him maybe two postcards in my lifetime, partly because my handwriting sucks, though I sent him a pretty great vintage postcard I ran across in Florida this last August. Most of my communication is done over email. I do write periodically to some other writers, too, and have started to embrace that process, partly for its pleasing formality and again its physicality. (I have a pad designed for telegrams that I like to use to send around, but for me writing other people is less about the writing and more about what I write on or with. I like collage; I like old forms and stationeries.)

Martone is always engaged in one project or another, usually manifesting themselves in physical ways (postcards, his small press, his many anthologies and books), and that polyamory has been an inspiration to me, though the term *inspiration* has been leached of much of its meaning by the self-help, feel-good culture of the last couple decades in America, and I hate to use the dying term. Still ... at the least we are fellow travelers in this particular way of engaging with the world.

I received a very strange package in the mail six months ago, potentially in response to a project I was asking friends to do for my thirty-third birthday: to make me a mix CD as a birthday present. I had hoped to get thirty-three, as a kind of record of that third of life, or whatever it is. Word got around and I got a lot of them, more than fifty, some from really random people whom I had not contacted. A standard business-size envelope appeared in the mail one day with no return address, addressed to me in handwriting I did not recognize. The postmark was from Nebraska City, Nebraska, which of course seems like a fake city, but it turns out it is a real city, real enough anyhow to be on Google Maps and to have its own Wikipedia page, and it looks to be a nice Nebraskan small town, and the official home of Arbor Day through some confluence of history and trees which I do not believe Nebraska is otherwise famous for. The envelope contained a microcassette that had been smashed in transit (or possibly smashed before transit) so it was unplayable. It sat on my shelf as I tried to figure out what to do with it. I didn't have a microcassette player, and the tape itself—the magnetic tape, not the case—was undamaged. I bought a blank microcassette in order to transplant the tape into a fresh body to make it again playable, but it resisted my abilities to lever the thing open. Because I did not know who had sent the tape, and because none of my friends, when queried, copped to it, I felt I had a real mystery on my hands. I finally ended up sending the thing away to a tape repair place I found online, and for a piddling forty-five dollars had the thing transplanted into a new body, and also burned to a CD so I could more easily listen to it. I brought the CD on an airplane (I forget where exactly I was en route to) and popped it in my computer to listen to with earbuds. The story goes on longer here, but here's what I found: the tape consists of recordings of one character's dialogue from the film version of the novel *Anatomy of a Murder*, the only film I can think of offhand (aside from the ludicrous Ben Affleck action flick *Reindeer Games*) that is filmed, and set, in the Upper Peninsula of Michigan, where I'm from. The recording is of the comments made by the judge character during the murder trial, responding, mostly to objections and arguments made by the lawyer characters, one played by Jimmy Stewart, and one played by George C. Scott. I had not, at the time, seen the film, so I didn't recognize the dialogue, nor the character names, and the whole experience of it had me a little bit freaked out because I had written in *Other Electricities* about a murder, a real-life murder (albeit fictionalized) in Upper Michigan. And the circumstances of the package's arrival were almost verbatim from what you'd expect of a murder-mystery type of novel.

I still have no idea who sent the tape, who bothered to record (and edit, apparently, which took some work, since the recording is indeed clean) just the judge's lines. And what this has to do with me, obviously, is not entirely clear. Am I the judge? Is the sender of the package the judge? And why was it sent from Nebraska City, Nebraska? And why on microcassette? And why unmarked and unlabeled and unpadded in a plain envelope? There are mysteries in this world, quite obviously, and this is one of them. I think, mainly because of the Nebraska City, Nebraska, postmark, that it is about 20 percent possible that this was sent to me by Martone on one of his jags through the Midwest. Which is to say I don't know this is true by any means, and I haven't asked him, and partly I'd prefer not to, to maintain the possibility that Martone, who is a trickster character in thought if not always in action, is responsible for this strangeness. And that is what being friends with the writer and person Michael Martone means, that a lot of things are possible, even if they are not always true.

....

Your concept that "a poem or painting or landscape is beautiful at the moment it is forgotten" reminds me of how my friend Juliet described her initiation as a Zen monk. After days of silent sitting at a monastery in Carmel Valley, California, she described her thoughts as oil and her mind as the water they slid off. Though the image implies peace, she assured me that it was a tremendous confrontation, which makes me wonder if your concept of the forgotten moment suggests, as Rilke says, that beauty is the beginning of terror.

Tan Lin: No, there is no terror in my writing, unfortunately. Terror implies, I think, some sort of surprise and I don't think a system such as poetry is capable of surprising itself. It is, after all, ambient. Its surprises are nonredundant communications that keep the system going.

•••••• ••••• ••

Does an agent of communication who keeps the system going differ from an interested party who assigns meaning?

Tan Lin: Yes, communication as a process is different. Communication seeks further communication. Laura (Riding) Jackson believed that further communication could be refined and directed, teleologically, to something she believed was the truth. The communications model is much more circular, ambient, and roundabout. We read in circles, not in straight lines. I just think that's the way we actually read. Honestly—who reads to get the truth?

•••••• ••••• ••

You have written that there are two kinds of power. "One is power *over*, held in place by victimization and oppression. The other power is *personal* power, the ability to make one's life go well, to make good decisions." How have you strived in your life to acquire the latter and resist the former?

Janisse Ray: As a child, as a female child, as a Southern child, as a poor child, I experienced a lot of "power over." That kind of power is unpleasant, at best, for the person on the bottom. At its worst it's violent, tragic, fatal.

I could also see the ways that I, being white (actually a very light brown!) and being educated, was on the upper levels of this ladder. That space, for me, was equally unpleasant.

The power that I've always believed in and tried to develop is personal power, but it is impossible to talk about power without talking about shame, because shame is one of the ways that we keep people from power. If you shame a person of color enough, or if you shame a woman enough, or a child enough, they internalize oppression, and internalized oppression doesn't resist; it doesn't act out. To be born into our current society is to be given a cross to bear, which is to figure out how to own your personal power without wounding anyone else, without wielding authority over anyone else.

....

You demonstrate the complexities of class anger through your characters.

Dorothy Allison: I remember reading a lot of writers from the thirties who were particularly expressive of class struggles, I suppose because of the Communist movement. In particular I loved the stories and poems by Meridel Le Sueur, who had a way of writing about class that was human and outrageous and wonderful. I sort of took her as a model.

What seemed to me lifesaving was that I couldn't lie. I couldn't put a candy-coated gloss on anything. In *Bastard*, for instance, there is a section where I give you a quick glimpse of Bone's Uncle Earle, and Bone loves her Uncle Earle, and he is charming as a motherfucker, but there is one paragraph where I let you see how angry and dangerous he is. She asks him, "What do you do if … ?" and he shows her the blade he has palmed and is hiding in his hand, and she sees the look in his eyes and senses his power. That's class. Trying to write with love and respect about people who even as you love them are destroying themselves and to try to write it accurately and with some of the grace of Meridel Le Sueur is the challenge. But you can't write about this stuff and be boring. That would be a sin against God.

•••••••••••

Do you think the capacity to empathize with human pain and fear equips people to access the contrary depths of love and joy?

Brandon Lingle: Captain Sean Ruane, an Air Force helicopter pilot I worked with in Afghanistan last year, said in an interview conducted by National Geographic during the deployment, "As a kid, war is something, you know, you run around your yard playing with your friends when you're six or seven with your toy guns. I guess being over here you realize how real it is. You appreciate life a lot more. Being able to sit on the couch with your wife and watch a movie becomes an amazing thing when you get home because you realize how quickly that can disappear over here." Just a few months after returning home from Afghanistan, Sean died in a helicopter crash with three other Airmen.

Sean's words stay with me. Combined with the knowledge that he's gone those words reinforce the point that personal narratives are the most important way to comprehend the effects of war and suffering. So, yes, I think the capacity to empathize with pain and death does open doors to the beauty and range of joy.

During deployments I'm aware of how valuable life is and how vulnerable we are in this world. When I get home from these trips, life becomes more vibrant and I appreciate the little things much more, but this urgency can fade with the doldrums of day-to-day life. When I return from my current deployment, I'll do everything I can to maintain such an appreciation. Hopefully, my essays can offer a similar reminder for the reader.

••••••••••••

What is something your father has done that you never could?

David Baker: He dropped out of high school. He served in the Merchant Marines, the Army, and the Air Force. (I was born at the Dow Air Force Base in Bangor, Maine.) He can survey a plot of land with the Geodolite and a rod, and he can convert those figures into contours, and he can turn those contours into actual graphs; he can take those graphs and sync them with aerial photographs and then make a finished map of the whole thing. I helped him do all that when I was a kid, but mostly I held the rod, and wrote the numbers down, and watched him use the Kelch machine and 3D glasses to draw the maps.

He can skin and field-dress any manner of animals or fish. On and on. He is hands-on, outdoors, improvised, make-do, fix-'er-up, and count-twice-cut-once.

•••·····••··

You write that the working-class hero is "invariably male, righteously indignant, and inhumanly noble." What defines a working-class heroine?

Dorothy Allison: That's much more complicated. When I was growing up, the portraits I found of working-class people were always very animalistic. The characters were portrayed as violent, physically dangerous, not very bright, and unreasonably angry, as if there were no reason for their anger. When I write these characters, I try to take you inside what it feels like to be treated with contempt and to have such a narrow range of possibilities for getting out.

That no-way-out is really the difference between boys and girls in working-class culture, because a working-class boy could run, or could when I was growing up. He could go west and change his name and start a new life for himself, and I know boys in my family did that. There is nowhere a girl can go. The only runaway position is prostitution, and that can kill you about as fast as a violent uncle or a crazy daddy.

I've got one cousin who went the other way, and me, and that's also complicated to talk about, because we were really smart. To realize at an early age that you're smarter than most of the people around you is scary. The only person I knew then who was smarter than me was my mama and she was so damaged that there wasn't a lot she could do with it. But she used to tell me, "You can do anything." Now that was not true, and I knew it wasn't true, but I also knew I was smart enough that there was a place I could go. The tragic cost of that is that it removes you from your own family.

Here's something I've never gotten over. When I was in sixth grade, they did IQ tests. In Greenville, South Carolina, just before we moved to Florida, I got the highest score in the school. They made me take the test over again, convinced I must have cheated, but I took it over and scored higher the second time. The message was "You're not the kind of person who's supposed to be scoring that high." They had an assembly where they gathered everybody in the gym to recognize the high scorers. That they did this still horrifies me, but they put me up there with the boy who had the second highest score and they treated us as if we had the same score. So the message is "You might be bright but don't get ahead of yourself."

It was almost like I was a boy, because I was being judged on intellect rather than the other standard for girls, which was to either marry well or to become a famously successful high-class whore. But the options for marrying well are limited, and if you're as angry and damaged as most working-class girls are you'll marry the first mean-assed boy who takes you up, so the next thing you know you have three babies and he's broken your jaw. They always break your jaw.

Instead, I went off and won scholarships. I applied for scholarships at church and ladies' circles. They're always service organizations run by middle-class women who are generous and kind to the poor. You win those awards by being humble and grateful. Gratitude can eat the heart out of you, because the first thing you have to do is acknowledge that you aren't as good as the people you're begging help from. That's one of the reasons why a lot of the very successful working-class kids who win scholarships drink themselves to death or shoot themselves in the head.

I know the damage. I can't even talk about it, because you're ashamed first because you had to beg and second because you had to treat your family very poorly. It's hurtful, and you're alone. When I go teach at small colleges, I try to get the working-class kids to get together for a meeting, and I say, "Look, I'm older than you. You will graduate. You need to go back home and make peace with your family. If you move into these people's world—with these people being the middle and upper class—you will always be one down unless you've got somebody at your back."

It is expensive, but it is a way out. I did it. I had one other cousin who did it. She became a pathologist. We were the only college graduates in my family. There weren't that many high school graduates. I was the first person in my family; she was the second.

By the time I was living in New York in my thirties there were six. The cost of growing up working class is an unacknowledged dam on society. We pretend we have an egalitarian society where you can move up if you work, but that doesn't mean shit if you go to the county farm or get pregnant at fifteen, and that's mostly what happens.

....

Is peacemaking something you did later?

Dorothy Allison: It is, and I was forced by circumstances. I don't think I would have listened to anybody who would have told me.

....

What circumstances?

Dorothy Allison: The point at which I started to publish and to win awards coincided with work I was doing for the Lesbian Sex Mafia. I was in New York City and working on the Sex and the Scholar Conference at Columbia University. We got picketed by Women Against Pornography. There were six of us they targeted, and we were called Pimps for the Pornographers, because we were feminists writing about sexuality.

They went after us like dogs after the conference, which blew up and became a huge fight within the feminist movement. People

I'd known for years would cross the street to avoid me. One of the other women who got caught in that horrific situation killed herself. All of a sudden I lost the family in the women's community I'd been building for a decade, which had become a substitute for the family I'd essentially lost.

When that happened, it coincided with my mother having a recurrence of cancer, so I went home to try to help take care of her. I was on the verge of collapse, but what I discovered is that when you do go home, they're ready. My sisters didn't like that I was writing about poverty and incest, but they also couldn't deny that it was the truth.

And I loved my mother. She had never walled herself off from me as I had walled myself off from her. I was ashamed of her. My waitress mother with her bleached blonde hair and her bright red lipstick and her high heels. The only books she read were murder mysteries. I wanted to be an intellectual and to have an intellectual mother, but instead I had my mom. There was a period of adjustment, but it revived my sense of pride in being working class. In addition to the outrage and anger there is that sense that we, my people, my tribe, are stronger and more resilient than anyone gives us credit for.

VI.

More Human than Humans

WHEN MY SECOND-grade teacher assigned our class to recite poetry, I knew immediately which poem I wanted to commit to memory. "There Once Was a Puffin" by Florence Page Jaques was my favorite from *A Child's Garden of Verses*, which my grandmother had given me. It tells the story of a seabird who, in a fit of loneliness, swears off eating fishes, "that were most delicious," in order to have someone to invite over for tea. I don't know if Jaques, who was born in Decatur, Illinois, had ever been to Vestmannaeyjar, an island off the coast of Iceland where puffins burrow beside "the bright blue sea" as in the poem. I hadn't, at seven, and didn't know that puffins themselves appear on menus there, and elsewhere, though the birds are endangered. Any animal-rights message inherent in the poem was lost on me. It was its music that drew me, and how the puffin felt lonely and small.

I too felt lonely and small when the other children began to recite their poems in the school library. My friend Stacy had chosen a poem by Edna St. Vincent Millay, which was not "Lament," but the effect of its opening lines was the same:

> Listen, children:
> Your father is dead.
> From his old coats
> I'll make you little jackets;

I'll make you little trousers

From his old pants.

The other kids had all gone adult overnight. The high-flown poems they had chosen depicted subjects as grave as death, so when my turn came, I felt I had no choice but to pull out another poem like a shield. It was shorter than the one I had planned but more serious. I hadn't even tried to memorize Emily Dickinson's "I Never Saw a Moor," I had simply internalized it, like the code of childhood that now betrayed me.

"I never spoke with God," Dickinson writes in the poem, which was precisely the problem. An omniscient advisor could better anticipate these upsets, and Google wouldn't be available to consult for years yet. Without an inside track, I was vulnerable to countless unknowns. It hardly mattered whether my favorite poem involved moors or puffins. I liked both better than those about battlefields or romance, but I would have memorized a grown-up poem had I known that's what we were doing. Tastes, I already knew, changed. Any preference I had at the time mattered little compared to kinship and belonging.

Plus, apart from the group, I never found myself to be anything fixed anyway. I tried to pin myself down to a singular source, one voice I recognized as mine, above those belonging to my mom, dad, teachers, and friends, but met only silence and blind space. Until I could figure out how to differentiate myself from that collective as well as the impenetrable shadow, I took comfort in a poet who found certainty in faith and human converse, and in any other available means of disguise that I didn't know myself yet.

If you had to narrow it down to one figurehead, whose likeness would you bear on your bow, and why?

Joe Hall: Joe Hill. It makes sense to put an itinerant person on the bow of a ship, my ship. And if I have to have a figurehead, I like Joe Hill because he didn't try to become a figurehead and most modern people wouldn't recognize him. Which maybe doesn't make him a figurehead. But at a certain point in time he was so dangerous as an Industrial Workers of the World martyr that the United States Postal Service seized an envelope with his ashes in it, considering these contents possibly subversive. These ashes eventually found their way into the National Archives and also Billy Bragg's stomach. Which seems about right. Having Joe Hill on my bow would also remind me to put my values in action outside the arena of the page. Otherwise, I'll never appear in a folk song. (Oh, I'll never appear in a folk song.)

....

Lately, I think of the checkout woman at my local grocery store, with her Coke-bottle glasses, as my guru. She squints and smiles, with her giant, magnified eyes. Do you have someone, or something, nearby that teaches you?

Michael Martone: If you look up my neighborhood on Google Earth—the streetscape pictures—you will see the woman who walks. There is a woman who walks back and forth through town every day. As she walks, she talks to God, sings, lectures. She is very striking. Tall, thin, gray hair, big unblinking eyes, an amazing wardrobe. I was so happy that, as the Google truck came down my street, she was walking. She always walks in the road and, as the truck goes by, she gives it the stink eye.

I think what I learn from her is a performance of the paradox: a bounded space contains an infinite amount of space. She walks from city limit to city limit, and yet this is not a dramatization of being trapped or cut off. It is the visual of the notion that the key to the treasure is the treasure, the journey and not the destination. She is finally present in a moment and each moment is liquid, sequential. She lives in each step.

·············

Do you follow any advice columnists?

Lia Purpura: I used to follow Dear Abby fanatically. In fact, my grandmother would send me huge packs of clipped columns when I was at college. Abby was sensible and no-nonsense ("Are you better off with him or without him?") and cut through the crap in really succinct ways. She was empathic, never coddled or scolded, and she wasn't above apologizing for a lousy answer or changing her point of view when presented with a better thought. And she had a kind of bawdy side, too. I wanted to *be* her—I very much wanted her job. She was—and this is rare now—an *adult*.

....

Your multimedia essay "drive, he sd" (after Robert Creeley's line) incorporates text from the last fifteen users on Twitter to use the hashtag #roadtrip. What does this unintentional collaboration add to each composition?

Eric LeMay: Surprise! I love that little piece, precisely because I never know what it's going to create. All of those road-trippers out there on the road, tweeting their high spirits. It's a take on that great American genre that lets the travelers themselves create the content—them and the Twitterbots tweeting back to them. So I suppose it's a collaboration among humans, yes, but also robots. I just triggered the essay, and I don't think the robot that tweeted "Priceline launched features for easier road trips for travelers" realized it had contributed to the literary arts. Otherwise, it would have corrected that clunky prose rhythm.

....

You describe writing as being similar to grooming, in that it involves "positioning, tweaking, adjusting . . . coloring slightly, rearranging, puffing up and patting down, all for the sake of effect." You question this process, even as you admit to loving it. What is it about grooming words that appeals to you?

Jane Tompkins: It's the ability to shape a piece that appeals, and the preparation to be seen that bothers me. I love the shaping partly because I've been doing it a long time and know how to do it pretty well. It's instinctive—lop off a piece here, put in a piece there, get rid of a whole swatch because it's tonally off, or a distraction, or just isn't written well. I recognize the intuitive nature of the process because I've recently started doing watercolors and don't have these instinctive responses in that medium, though I'm beginning to acquire a few after three years.

As for the part that worries me, the process of revision can seem intensely narcissistic. All that energy expended in order to get things to sound just right. Heaven forbid that anyone should think I was naive, dull, ham-fisted, maudlin, stuffy, etc. It's all about *me*. The analogy to cosmetics works. I notice when I'm putting on makeup that I am more completely absorbed than I am when doing most other things. It's not a particularly pleasant form of absorption. The process is usually accompanied by an unconscious stream of critical observation about my looks, frustration at not being able to do anything with my hair, annoyance at not having the right shade of lipstick yet again, exasperation at not having left enough time to do a good job, and so on. Revising prose is equally absorbing but a lot more fun. You can feel your muscles ripple, your energy rise. But it can turn nasty, too. Self-criticism is the most narcissistic part—masquerading as a just estimate of one's abilities.

....

Lately I've been reading plagiarists—amateurs who are trying to pass junior English, and professionals who employ it creatively. Have you ever plagiarized anything? What's your take on it?

Nicole Walker: I'm too chicken to plagiarize. Shame is one of my go-to emotions and I don't want to go there more than I have to, so I can't consciously plagiarize. But I love David Shields's *Reality Hunger*. At a very dark time in my life, I read that book and it lifted me because it was not all about the writer. It was all about the reader. How much pleasure can I give, Shields seem to ask, by putting together all the brilliance of a hundred years. It removed the ego of the writer and put words and meaning first. His pleasure, I predict, was in the offering, not that self-rewarding feeling of writing something that you imagine to be original and then fifty minutes later realize you heard this one before on another station.

....

If you and some friends were in a band, what would you name it?

Joe Hall: This happened. We were called Nanobots: A Rock Opera. We wrote about twenty songs. They were mostly folk songs about nanobots that built robots who were more human than humans.

•••••••• ••

How does a robot become more human than humans?

Joe Hall: This band was a collaboration with my friend Tom, so I always risk getting this wrong. Essentially, we agreed that humans have largely failed at being human. We're boring, insensitive, and egotistical. Once we identify ways to decrease our capacity to feel and think, we relentlessly pursue those ways. That's at least how humans are in the dystopic future-present of our folk-rock opera. So the more-human-than-human robots do the opposite. They feel and react to things in intense, fluid ways. They're also very folksy. Often the most sophisticated technology they use is themselves. But why try to explain this in prose? The lyrics of "Behind Robot Lines" speak for themselves. Here, a human who has infiltrated a robot family is reporting back on robot culture, in song, to the remaining humans:

> They're really earnest speakers
> They're jokers with their friends
> Most are good to their families
> Most look out for their kin
>
> They raise robot families
> They keep robot dogs

They write robot poetry
They live in robot nature
They cut robot logs

•••••••••••

Humor isn't listed as a noble truth in *The Mindful Writer: Noble Truths of the Writing Life*, but I know humor informs your writing and perhaps your Buddhism. Will you talk about your relationship to it?

Dinty W. Moore: Humor defines me. It is how I found my identity in the world. I remember cracking tiny jokes under my breath to impress my first-grade girlfriend, a freckled, buck-toothed girl with red plastic eyeglasses. The sound of her giggling, her smile when she turned slightly in the desk, was addictive. I couldn't get enough. Later, humor writers like Robert Benchley and Art Buchwald opened me up to the possibilities of writing with humor but still saying something worthwhile. Buddhism teaches us that our thoughts create our reality, that our world is constructed through the habitual way we find ourselves viewing life, so I view the world with a wry, fond smile. Not a bad place to be.

•••••••••••

In another interview, you say that rather than being known as a funny poet you would prefer to be known as a "totally-indifferent-to-angora poet." But let's face it, no one is totally indifferent to angora.

Bob Hicok: I'm not even sure what angora is. It's a word I like, and I know people make clothes out of it. I'll google it. This will take a minute—I had to turn the MiFi on. Now refresh the network. Again. There it is. Now to Google—oh my god—it's rabbit fur. I did not know. Those are some weird-looking rabbits. Angora sweaters would look really cool if they were made of the actual rabbits. A living sweater. Which would of course mean a shitting sweater. Thus ends my career in fashion.

···· ··· ··

How does taboo inform your sense of humor?

Gail Storey: When I taught inner-city kids for Writers in the Schools, a second grader once wrote that she liked my "sins of humor." I love to laugh, and I have more costumes than regular clothes in my closet. I try to be a good steward of my life, I take the privilege of the human experience quite seriously, but I don't take the small, conditioned self all that seriously. So my "sins of humor" are a way of saying to that small self, it's okay, honey, just relax in the deep "Don't Know."

···· ··· ··

What's your most unexpected go-to sacred text?

Dinty W. Moore: There is the fine moment in *A Night in Casablanca* when Groucho Marx gives orders to the restaurant staff: "We've got to speed things up in this hotel. If a guest orders a three-minute egg, give it to him in two minutes. If he orders a two-minute egg, give it to him in one minute. If he orders a one-minute egg, give him a chicken and let him work it out for himself." Now that's a worthy koan.

....

Do you have a favorite joke?

Coleman Barks: Two caterpillars walking along talking. A butterfly comes along overhead. One caterpillar turns to the other: "You'll never get me up in one of those things."

....

Your poems suggest that you might laugh at those, including yourself, who take themselves too seriously. What is your favorite joke?

Bob Hicok: I. Can't. Remember. Or. Tell. Jokes. To. Save. My. Life. Or. The. Life. Of. A. Fly. I'm not a fan of jokes, per se. I liked Richard Pryor, who didn't tell jokes so much as the truth. And ran while on fire. Wow. And then made that funny.

....

Have you ever run while on fire? Or set fire to the truth? Or doused the truth with baking soda, and run?

Bob Hicok: No. It sounds like I've lived a sheltered life. Or not baked enough.

....

I recognize moments of what Wallace Stevens calls "la nonchalance divine" in your work. What is the function of levity in writing?

Ellen Doré Watson: Let's see . . . maybe I wake from emotional bedlam with a can of spray-starch in my hand—an unconscious survival strategy? Seriously, though, I think levity is as elemental to human experience as grief. It's very American to assume darkness and light to be separate realms, as reflected in most Hollywood movies, where one or the other is magnified to the point that the result is black and white in Technicolor: broad, shallow comedy or a riot of fear and violence, neither of which bears much resemblance to life as we know it. And life as we know it requires humor—and not simply as a cordoned-off moment of relief. Which is why I love Pedro Almodóvar, for example, whose films satisfy so deeply precisely because they reflect the very short distance between tears and laughter.

•••••·••••••

When in your life have you felt freest?

Raven Jackson: I feel the freest around water. Most of my films involve it in some capacity. My feature project revolves around a protagonist who can't swim. Neither can I. As I work toward completing the project, I plan to also take swimming lessons. It feels right. To also go on this journey with the film. Water is every- where. On the pages of my script. In the images. It feels right to have it on me, too. To learn how to swim alongside my protagonist.

•••••·••••••

What's the most categorically unspiritual of your go-to sacred texts?

Brenda Miller: *Charlotte's Web*. Now some would call this a blatantly spiritual text, but I never noticed it until a few months ago. All I knew was that I carried this book around with me since the time I was seven. It made it into every moving box, onto every bookshelf. I remember its torn cover giving me comfort in the tiny studio apartment I rented as a graduate student in Missoula, Montana. The apartment building dated from the turn of the century, and each apartment had a cunning little bed that slipped into the sideboard like a drawer. I don't think the mattress had been changed in all that time. I'd lie on that musty mattress, looking up at the few books on the shelf in that cupboard, wondering if I could ever really be a writer. Charlotte would always be there, spinning her words of wisdom above me. I memorized the closing lines, in which Wilbur muses: "It is not often that someone comes along who is a true friend and a good writer. Charlotte was both." I think I'd always taken that as a directive, to be a true friend and a good writer, and maybe I've accomplished at least one of those mandates.

•••••••••

If you could have a conversation with any writer living or dead, what would you ask?

Dinty W. Moore: Does Jesus count? I'd like to ask him, "Did we get any of it right, or did organized religion screw up absolutely everything you were trying to say?"

•••••••••

What is the best writing advice you've ever gotten?

Gail Storey: Grace Paley read some of my early writing and said, "You're okay, kid, even when you're foolin' around." I took that as reassurance that my full writer could show up in all her extremes from the sexual to the spiritual, the serious to the outrageously comic.

···········

Will you talk about the dawning of your sexuality? Were there models you followed, sought, resisted, or reinvented?

Marc Gaba: It's a very sad image, a young teenager chanting "I am straight" before a mirror, repeating it until exhausted, hoping for effect. Sadder and worse, that I attempted to lure women—beautiful, intelligent ones—into my delusion that I could alter my sexuality, until I turned twenty-one and knew there was no hope of changing, and I almost killed myself: I sincerely believed by then that there was no happiness for me in the future (and I was right, romantically, but it's no reason to die) because I would lose my family. I've felt great kinship with Bishop's position: love who you love, live it, and keep it out of poetics, but not out of poetry. When literature opened fully to gay voices and it turned into something to wear, I resisted, because I think that homosexuality as *image*, as *the represented*, has nothing beyond cultural value, and drag to me is a drag; it's not even sexual, and disco is something else. I used to think, "I'm not gay, I'm ancient Greek." Because it's my body's honest craving.

I had a crush on Frank O'Hara, but that doesn't make him a model. His sexuality was about freedom: his sexuality was sexy. And beautiful love poems—pure ones—came out of him, too. I'm gushing, it's disgusting. Anyway: it wasn't quite modeling that happened. You know I don't like putting people in boxes like *Asian American studies*, and I hope to God that this thinking isn't going exclusively to *queer studies*: it would be unfair. Which could mean that Elizabeth Bishop must have been my model. Yep, this faggot's model is a lesbian. But that said, Hopkins, the first modern poet in Anglo-American literature, warmed me to Bishop, and Michele Glazer's work showed me an ethical problem of Bishop's metaphorizing. In brief: inscape and instress: now and forever.

·········· ··

Was the ethical problem inherent to Bishop in particular, or to metaphorizing in general?

Marc Gaba: Metaphorizing a human being is inherently unethical, I think. To be fair, Bishop was describing an old fish, but what she likens it to becomes what one sees and thinks about: the human being, the veteran. It's anthropomorphizing, sure, but by the second line ("[she] held him beside the boat"), it's too emotionally clear to me that she's dealing with someone other than the fish. Fishy, all too fishy. The poem has hundreds of other aspects that a self-respecting reader can certainly bring up to defend Bishop's "The Fish"—for instance, that the poem is aware, too, of the problem insofar as it's about perception and cognition—but nothing can erase the fact that the central action of the poem is the metaphorizing gaze.

·········· ··

I know people can commune with one another who have not shared a particular experience, but must empathy be earned? If so, how, and are there limits to empathy?

Wendy S. Walters: I suspect everything good connected to other people must be earned, consciously or unconsciously. But as far as empathy goes, I am not sure everyone has that in them. I am not certain everyone should. In lieu of empathy a certain set of personal ethics would do, but many people don't even have that to call on. Personal ethics can be employed at any moment, and if maintained with some consistency, I think they can be more effective than empathy. That said, I think it's unhelpful to mock people who experience a lot of feeling for others. They can't help this anymore than those who don't have feeling naturally come to them.

....

How does integrating various voices, like Sei Shōnagon's and Stephen Jay Gould's, inspire your work?

Kimiko Hahn: I've been called a magpie as far as range of subject and reference go. My first draw is usually language, which is certainly the case with Gould. The language of science is so exotic to my ear. Sei Shōnagon's pillow book offers form, such as the list, and a subjectivity that is tantamount to self-mythologizing. I love that.

....

What rules has the writing life subjected you to?

Nicole Walker: Other people's rules. Everything I do is fast. The writing world can be a slow place. Patience to revise. Patience to submit work. Patience to look around and see how caterpillars really move (humpy) and how ravens scavenge (not always: I saw one kill a pigeon). If there's one way that writing makes me a better human, it reminds me to be patient. As I write more and begin to imagine a more generous way to write, I am beginning to live under, if not the rules of the audience, at least the idea of what one might be interested in reading. I want to inhabit the space of the audience. That way, I get to be two people at once—writer and reader. And another reader sometimes. It's the way I imagine living longer— being multiple people. Maybe even multiple patient people.

....

Have you ever had a dream about an octopus?

John Domini: My family comes from Naples, Italy, where the octopus of the Gulf has been a totemic figure for millennia, not to mention a delicious dish that can be had cheaply—a common delicacy, you might say—all over the greater metro area. Above my desk as I type sits a freestanding wooden rendering of an octopus, a stylization in lovely golden-brown walnut, and who cares that I found it on the island of Kauai? Among Neapolitans, too, many local proverbs derive their significance from the octopus. Perhaps the most resonant remains *O puolpo si ccuocce in accua sua*, "The octopus cooks in its own water," a saying with a dozen meanings at least, having to do with everything from love to criminality. The storylines tentacle out everywhere.

··········

How do you see the role of a writer who teaches?

Ellen Doré Watson: I think the poet-teacher's job (as in translation) is to resist every temptation to "direct" the performance/text, twisting it in the direction she most values, and instead to discern its intrinsic intentions, and (unlike translation) to identify its possible pivot points. But it is equally important for her to inspire students to read constantly, widely, deeply—both in and away from their comfort zones.

··········

In your essay "Recurrences/Concurrences," you mention a teacher friend who disarms students by handing out obituaries. Is there something that similarly disarms you?

Lia Purpura: I can give you an entire list in a single phrase: "That could be you." The sensation that, very much like the Road

Runner, we're all constantly and unconsciously dodging falling anvils, all over the place. And that I'd better be aware/grateful that my life has been mostly Road Runner and not so much Wile E. Coyote. As Nabokov said, "A thrill of gratitude to whom it may concern." The near-miss nature of it all ...

VII.

Atomic Bonds

THE AFTERNOON THAT the spider outside my window spun her expansive web, thunder shook the air. Clouds rolled in, and I went outside to see what the spider would do. The silk trembled in the wind, but she was nowhere to be seen. I thought she might have dropped to the ground, until I spotted her under the eave. Rain began to pelt. From inside, I watched the web glisten and fall. The spider watched, too, presumably, with the eight eyes that orb weavers have, although I couldn't see her eyes from the window. I could see only the dome of her abdomen as she sat under the lip of the house. Her relative size and short lifespan emphasized the significance of her lost labor. I wondered that she'd chosen an unprotected space, when there were canopies of trees nearby, and a day of torrential rain to spin her web. Apparently, spiders had no sixth sense for barometric pressure.

How would she make it with her luminous net laid to waste in the grass? I thought of Job's servants running back "alone escaped" to tell him that his house, his sons and daughters, his livestock, were destroyed. In the sunlight the web had looked nothing short of miraculous.

I thought of that broken web again, when I had nearly finished this essay and one of my interviewees retracted their contributions, a trans writer. Distraught, I deleted their ten answers and our three months of work. I apologized, uncomprehending what had happened, then sat in heavy silence. I had come to think of them as the book's conscience, since they raised points that no one else had.

When I relayed the turn of events to my friend Mechele, she suggested that retracting the interview might have served them as a safe opportunity to establish boundaries. Since our interview promoted the release of a revealing book, which offered readers access that might be uncomfortable as it moved beyond the page, Mechele's rationale made sense and gave me hope that our exchange had not been for naught.

To justify her logic, Mechele shared a story about a time when she worked for a printing company in the 1990s. Although we had known each other for almost a decade, she had never told me about Allen, one of the workers she managed, who transitioned to Aileen while under her supervision. Mechele said she had to protect Aileen from her coworkers even though many of them, like her, were gay and had themselves been bullied and deemed wrong by society. When Mechele left that job and could no longer help Aileen hold the space she had claimed, her coworkers forced her to go back to being Allen.

Thinking of Aileen reminded her of another story, one even more painful to recall. "P-Knutts was beautiful," she said, using the stage name for her friend Jerry Cope, who was killed in 1992. "She had long red hair that she would flip over her shoulder and say, 'Honey, buy me a cocktail.'" Jerry worked at a local bar, the Brown Derby. "Bars were the only place in town you could go and feel accepted, before the proliferation of social media," she said.

P-Knutts had only worked at the bar for two weekends when she had her throat slit at the end of her shift. According to a newspaper article about the murder, there were two sets of footprints in her blood, a pair of tennis shoes and a pair of cowboy boots, but no one was ever prosecuted.

"Sometimes I forget what I've been through," Mechele said, having raised a son with another woman and having had her own life endangered on multiple occasions.

Shaken by these offered accounts, I imagined I could relate. Although I had never lived such threats directly, I was conditioned by writers, artists, pastors, and other teachers to empower the imagination to empathize with others' experiences. Yet that broken premise confuses empathy with trespass. In fact, empathy is involuntary, vulnerable-making, and intentional only insofar as we relinquish any illusions of power in the face of situations we cannot change. Together, Mechele and the retracting interviewee had shown me that, although I might find countless points of comparison to relate to trans writers, Aileen, P-Knutts, and others, including orb-weaving spiders, they were not coordinates. I could not navigate where they led, deep into experiences I could not know, at the limits of the imagination they had been bold enough to bare.

Your painting *Mother and Child* displays two clean-lined silhouettes one would not immediately identify as a mother and child. A woman strides unaccompanied toward some agenda, a sheaf of papers in hand, while a middle-aged man in an overcoat prepares to pass her—a businessman, judging by his briefcase. Adults both. Equals perhaps, although the man is closest to viewers in the frame—his head serving as the apex of the compositional pyramid.

Marc Gaba: The woman was really intended to be the mother, and the child the grown man. The title came much later. It was untitled for the longest time. When I was thinking about the show, I realized what the title should be. There's a convention that is especially popular in the Philippines, a kind of subgenre of "Mother and Child" paintings that usually depict a mother with a baby. So I was thinking of it as a kind of update—that just because the child is grown doesn't mean that he is no longer a child. And, as you've pointed out, the man is closer to us, which is almost an exaggeration of his having grown up.

But one thing that I want to point out is that they belong to different perspectives in the physical world, that they are not subject to a single perspective. They are subject to the flatness of the paint, but that visual configuration of them is impossible in real life, which is just to say that these two figures are subject to their individual perspectives, which they carry with them. Their relationship is shared, but their perspectives as individuals in that relationship are different and always will be.

....

Would you say that *Postcapitalism*, the series to which *Mother and Child* belongs, heralds a world in which people, including artists, are freed from assumptions implied by identity taglines? Because that's not "how the public likes its artists," Rilke says in his diaries—as if there were enough fright and menace in life itself, without allowing people, too, to be limitless.

Marc Gaba: I wouldn't say that *Postcapitalism* "heralds" such a world, but it hopes for that kind of world, and perhaps naively suggests questions toward it, while also understanding that it could be either impossible or already in the world as possibility or as moments of complexly luminous perception. As far as it actively dreams of such a world, Rilke must be right—that is not how the public likes its artists, but we're not supposed to give the public what the public wants all the time. Almost never should we do that. It's not a beauty contest; it's not an election. That's not what artists are for. I think it is especially important now because capitalism has gotten to be so large and personally invasive that people are reduced to their taglines, which is a reduction that artists know is simply false. As for there being more than enough fright and menace in life itself, there's a difference between a limit and a narrowness, and I think so long as we're aware of that distinction, then we don't have to be frightened or menaced by how much we can see.

•••·····••··

Will you say more about how your family influences your creative work?

Raven Jackson: On a recent trip to Mississippi, I sat with my grandma, mother, aunt, and cousin—among other family—looking through photo albums. It felt like we were conjuring up years gone past and, in many ways, we were. Family's a hinge for my work. I'm interested in the ways familial relationships shift and bloom. The scars. The growth.

Filming *all dirt roads taste of salt* was a catalyst to interview family members, but the interview process feeds me in other ways. It illuminates memories and details of people I love. I remember speaking with my father about how, in his youth, in Alabama, he'd often fight white boys in school who'd call him "nigger." Sometimes, they'd follow him as he walked home, by railroad tracks. When my father hid a weapon inside of a washer, grabbed it after school, and waited for the boys on his walk home, a preacher stopped him before anything could escalate.

This experience—of my young father—made it into some of my poems, and now lives inside my film. It feels organic, the conversation being had between experiences of family and the film. But delicate, too, and vulnerable. Even though *all dirt roads taste of salt* is fiction, it's a priority of mine to get at the emotional weight of familial experiences and details I use in the film. It's almost another way to name them.

....

How have forests informed your sense of individuality?

David Haskell: First they have informed my understanding of death. Biologically, the line between life and death is not so clear for these networked giants. When a tree falls its life in the network continues, albeit in an increasingly decentralized way.

The forest is a living network where "individuality" is a temporary manifestation of relationships. Networks of interconnection persist, evolve, and are the fundamental biological "ground" of being in the forest, not "selves." I mean that not in a mystical way, but as a reality incarnate in the genetics, physiology, and ecology of all creatures. The same is true of the "human" body which is, in fact, a living community of thousands of species of bacteria, fungi, and larger "human" cells that are themselves aggregations of formerly free-living bacteria. Our culture takes this to another level: the social nature of humans means that most ideas live in the networked relationships among people, not in "individual" minds.

....

How does your scientific background practice you in making comparisons?

David Haskell: Most of science is metaphor: words and images that we use to imagine what our senses cannot apprehend. Atomic bonds. Evolutionary trees. Photons. Cycles of carbon and phosphorous. A metaphor is only helpful, though, if it emerges from experience. Otherwise it is merely clever. In science experience is often highly organized into experimental investigations, but sometimes experience is more informal and qualitative. In my writing I try to integrate what we've learned from experiments and other organized forms of investigation with the day-to-day experience of a tree or a patch of woodland. Metaphors help to build that bridge. I use connections that resonate with both my understanding of the science and my experience in the field. Our educational system sometimes teaches us that metaphor and imagination belong in the humanities and "facts" belong in the sciences. The human mind, though, is not divided, so such divisions seem absurd to me.

....

Do you think of the language of science as a form of translation?

Kimiko Hahn: For me, personally, the language is part narcotic, part portal. Perhaps those are aspects of translation.

....

I love your description of garba, a dance form that originated in India. You say: "Everyone forms a circle, moving right then left, changing direction, clapping and turning. Picture sea anemones washing first in toward the shore, then out, following the water, the graceful movement of a wave." Do you think group dances shape interpersonal relationships—and if so, how?

Sejal Shah: The image of sea anemones is taken from Chitra Banerjee Divakaruni's poem "Garba." Both garba and raas are from the state of Gujarat, where my father grew up and also where my mother's family is originally from. These are group folk dances drawing people of all ages, performed every fall for Navaratri, the fall harvest festival, and at weddings. Garba was always about dancing with my female friends from elementary school onward—and there was some competitiveness, learning new steps or flourishes. We would practice off to the side in the cafeteria or outside the gym (Navaratri was always held at a high school gym, two weekends in the fall).

What I especially appreciate about raas is that there is a specific pattern and also that you play dandiya or hit sticks in this pattern with every other person in the circle opposite from you. Imagine two concentric circles facing each other. As the circles turn in opposite directions, you are dancing with people whose names you will not know—there's something about civic engagement and community for me in that you make eye contact, greet each other, acknowledge. When we were young you might warn your friends, Look out for that auntie, she hits the dandiya hard or smashes your hands sometimes, or that uncle doesn't really hit at all, just taps the air.

My husband, who is Tamil, doesn't have that same sense of being part of a community I notice the Gujarati kids in our community had, and that I connect in part to dancing with them at Navaratri. The closest American dance I can think of to garba or raas is square dancing. When I lived in Iowa, I went with friends I made in town to a dance with the Foot-Notes—a local band that played Norwegian American dances. I only lived in Iowa for a year, but dancing forged a stronger connection to the local community and culture.

•·········••

What are you going to do after this interview?

Marc Gaba: I'm going to work on a painting. I think I hit upon a solution to introduce narrative to the process. As far as creation goes, that's the best thing that's happened today. I found where in that abstraction is the beginning and the end. Of course, it's going to be a process, because in abstract painting, to finish is to make narrativity disappear.

•·········••

That's a nice line.

Marc Gaba: Thank you. I think abstract paintings work when you can enter from any point and it takes you somewhere as your eye moves around the frame. I always love that moment. The image comes from a Jorie Graham poem in her book *Swarm*, which I would recommend to anyone going through a transition. She is knocking on a door, and the tone of the poem tells you that she has been knocking for a long time already, asking to be let in. I feel like these abstract paintings just suddenly open the door.

VIII.

The Hole that Will Be Left

"I'D TRADE MY masculinity for a Popsicle," my housemate Rob said, elbows akimbo behind his head topped with a black beanie. I was curled beside him on the futon and surrounded by Flomp, Michlich, and the four other guys who lived with us. Lee was perched cross-legged in the papasan. Nathan flanked him in a purple recliner.

After my only sibling died of cancer at twenty, I had circled back to Boulder, where I had been in graduate school when he was diagnosed two years before. Friends of friends had an empty room, and soon my climbing mat was unrolled on its floor. They were all about my brother's age, six years younger than me. The dynamic felt natural, since I had spent the previous year in my Virginia hometown with my brother and his friends while he underwent medical treatment, my own friends gone or more settled. At times it even seemed I could make up for lost time with him through them.

The guys and I spent a lot of time the way my brother, his friends, and I had—gathered around a stereo in the living room, except the music differed in Colorado, with Yonder Mountain String Band and Spearhead cycling through the selections instead of Jay-Z and Johnny Cash.

I laughed so hard at Rob's dismissal of his masculinity that I ached to call my brother and repeat it to him. Naturally he had no takers, since the only American ideal these boys romanticized was that of the lawless frontier, which Coloradans had long since traded in on the cowboy. Instead, they glorified the increasingly gender-neutral figures of ski bums, backcountry guides, and wilderness survivalists. Every week as many unwashed girls as boys emerged from their tents in the mountains to use our shower and stock up on staple goods. But Rob's offer was so close to a trade Jeremy would suggest while he was in the hospital, to request a Mountain Dew Slurpee or chocolate milk, I wondered if he had put those words in Rob's mouth. Before my brother died, he had promised to interact with us on earth.

"I'm not sure how it works," Jeremy had said one night when we were talking after our parents had gone to bed. By that point, his cancer had metastasized, and several additional surgeries had not eliminated it. "But, if I can come back as a ghost or whatever, I'm going to have fun with it, like walk through walls and mess with people, so be ready."

"We should plan something specific, so I'll know it's you," I suggested.

"Like turn your TV upside down?" he asked. I nodded. "But what if I can't lift heavy things?"

He wanted to do me a favor, like find lost car keys or a missing wallet, but we couldn't settle on a place to put them that would be obvious yet unexpected, since I didn't know where I would live in a year, and he didn't want to scare Mom. Every prospect was so sad I had to hold my sorrow away from myself like a caught fish, without thinking about the hook ripping through its innards.

Being nearly seven years older positioned me in most of our talks as the advising sibling. I had helped teach him how to read, swim, and hike in the forest behind our house. I taught him how to fold a grass stem to shoot its seed head like a pop gun and where to plant his feet on the slippery shale bank. There were skills he surpassed me at, like gleeking and gaming, but when it came to the ways of the world, he looked to me as the forerunner. Yet what did I know of the terror that the most aggressive chemotherapy available couldn't cure me? In the years after he slipped on a treadmill and came home from the doctor's office with a bone tumor, he became the knowing one. I could offer little in the way of insight, but I could steel myself to listen as he processed dire medical news.

"I'll figure out a way to connect," he decided. "Hopefully you'll be able to tell."

A rainbow filled the sky on the morning that Jeremy died. My heart was far too heavy to lift as we walked to meet the ambulance that would carry him away, but deep down I knew a line of communication had opened.

On one of our ventures into the woods around our house, Jeremy pointed out his favorite color overhead, a deep cerulean blue between azure and cobalt. I studied it with the forget-me-nots blooming on the creek bank, swallowtails outspreading on the fence posts, cardinals swooping between the green canopies of trees, but I liked all of the shades and told him I couldn't choose.

In the years that followed his death, I developed a theory of the afterlife based loosely on Newton's first law of thermodynamics, which states that nothing can be created or destroyed but only changes form. It comforted me to think physics would seem to allow the energy that comprised my brother still to exist. I think of that energy sometimes as awareness, and sometimes as will, which is to say at times I conflate my lost brother with God. I can be certain, at least, my brother is sympathetic.

Before I comforted myself with that theory, though, I had only his absence, which I mourned with jokes he would never crack, barbecued chicken legs he could no longer eat, weddings he would not attend, nieces or nephews I would not have. When I met those Colorado boys who never got to know him but were so lighthearted he might have picked them out for me, to encourage me to laugh again, I imagined they were the nice thing, the misplaced keys or wallet, he wanted to return to me.

So I went with Rob when he decided to conduct an experiment to see if the sun could ever set yellow, rather than scatter into the electric pink and cyan sunsets we saw below the Flatirons. I stepped onto the running board of his pickup, which was outfitted with backcountry tires so enormous he had to reach across the cab to pull me inside.

At the top of Mount Sanitas, we sat on a rocky overlook and watched the light beat lemon, until shadows lengthened in the distant fields. Denver's skyline smudged bronze on the horizon, as the sky deepened to my brother's choice cerulean.

"I don't really have deep thoughts, but I have a lot of thoughts," Rob said.

The sun dipped lower in the sky but stayed yolky. Rob wished he had brought one of the eggs he had boiled, which had been sitting on the stove for several days in the pot he had used. I told him he shouldn't eat those because they hadn't been refrigerated, but he said, "You don't have to refrigerate eggs, because they're basically hermetically sealed."

"Rob, that's how you get salmonella!" I cried.

"Wow, I guess chicken shells aren't as strong as I thought," he said. I had to smile. Although I couldn't make sense of hardships I had seen in the hospital where babies' tiny chests bore catheters for chemo, I could appreciate that the same world had safeguarded this innocent.

When the sun was only a sliver of shimmering eyelid and still golden, Rob thought we had it first try, but minutes later the whole spectrum popped like canned biscuit dough and spilled lavender, rose, salmon, copper, across the Front Range.

"Want to try again tomorrow?" he asked, one hand extended to help me up. I did.

For weeks, every day when I got home from work, Rob went to his room, grabbed his keys, and nodded toward me, grinning at the prospect that this sunset would be the one. Daily he remained undaunted, sure that solid gold would happen, and we would be there to witness it. And daily I followed him, with a different hope altogether.

Every afternoon for weeks we barreled over curbs and out of the city, up the mountain, as if into the clouds, to look at the sun. Every day, it changed form. With each burst of yellow into viridian, indigo, violet, blush, Rob stood and extended a hand. The phenomenon was just beginning. The ultramarine outline of impending twilight had yet to snake through the valley, but we had today's answer, so we headed down.

Have you ever seen a ghost?

Rae Armantrout: I've never seen a ghost, but I've been haunted by the memory of my mother who died a painful death about twelve years ago. That may have something to do with the references to ghosts in my poems. But then, too, I've been interested in the portrayal of the "afterlife" in the mass media. For instance, there was a medium who had a TV show a few years back. He would guess at the identities of the dead relatives of his audience members and then he would give the chosen audience members a message from their dead relatives. I was struck by how similar the messages all sounded.

•••••••••••

Edmond Jabès writes in "The Book of the Absent" that "brotherhood means giving, giving, giving. And you can only give what you are." *Stealing History* is an example of your gift to brotherhood and sisterhood both. What would your belief in them cut us from or into?

Gerald Stern: It would cut us from complacency, blind obedience, stupid cooperation, and compromise. It would cut us away from specialization and secrecy. It would cut us away from billy clubs, and gas. Most of all, it would cut us away from The Lie. The brotherhood and sisterhood that you mention sometimes exists in words alone, in poems alone, but I think really that life is more important than art. Maybe it is absurd to separate them. I think basically that *Stealing History* has, as its underlying motif, this brotherhood and sisterhood, even if it is sometimes ruthless.

············

Fanny Howe writes, "One definition of lyric might be that it is a method of searching for something that can't be found." Did you conduct such a search with *Versed*?

Rae Armantrout: *Versed* is in two sections, "Versed" and "Dark Matter." The poems in "Dark Matter" and those at the end of "Versed" were written in the wake of a cancer diagnosis and surgery. That was almost three years ago, but, at the time, the prognosis was not good. I was searching (or I was forced to search) for ways to live with extreme uncertainty and for ways to imagine my own absence.

············

Do you feel straightened by that imagining, or see anything straighter because of it?

Rae Armantrout: I don't plan ahead as much as I used to. Even though I seem to be cancer-free, I feel like I've seen the end and I know it's there.

•••••••••••

Being a physician and writer must have exercised and tested your compassion over the years. Would you say that empathy can be trained?

Thomas Gibbs: I am writing you as I wait to take a woman to the operating room for a D&C after fetal demise. It will probably be midnight before the surgery and one or two before she goes home.

The staff here calls me a dinosaur, still in solo practice, hanging around late at night. But I have not given you a direct answer . . . I was twelve when my mother went down to my father's office for a pregnancy test. She was pregnant, but when the lab tech, (my Uncle George) looked at the blood smear he called my father to check. They saw the leukemia but could not tell her. The next day my father drove her up to the university medical center in Syracuse. It was fall and they stopped along the back roads of the Finger Lakes and took pictures of Mother standing in front of the autumn leaves.

I am not sure what the doctors told her about pregnancy and cancer. I remember her coming home. The family prayed for a miracle. My mother lived to deliver my sister Mary, the last of her ten children. At some point as the family fervently asked God to save her, I came to the realization that there would be no heavenly intervention. I got my driver's license the summer before she died. I put a mattress in the back of the station wagon, carried her down to the car and drove her around the lake. She loved the shore birds and herons. We would look for them in her favorite coves. By fall we listened to the Canada geese as they flew to a warmer place. When she fell asleep on the way home, I would sing to her.

•·······••

Mary Rose O'Reilley says, "To grow in compassion for one's own life is the great task of the middle years." What would you consider the task of the middle years to be?

David Keplinger: I consider the task of the middle years to be the same task as at any other time: to learn to serve others while serving, somehow, yourself, your own calling. The task of the middle years is still compassion, but it's got to begin to turn outward so that the self we begin to see is something larger than our poems, our reputation, our job, or our relationships. It's absolutely necessary. A great poet, and a brother to me, the late Jake Adam York, taught me that to fully engage with the work I can't spend all of my time contemplating Being. As Czesław Miłosz puts it, sometimes you're cornered by History. The work must grow to fit this larger sense of self. Or the fire will go out.

•·······••

There is an "ache of longing" in your translation of Rumi's Quatrain #320 that expresses a kind of wealth. Mulling and absorbing Rumi's lines as only you have must have led to an ache of wealth. If longing is a hidden wealth, what does a wealth of poems hide?

Coleman Barks: Good question. That hidden wealth metaphor comes up a lot in Rumi. When you demolish a building (the ego), there is a chance that you will find two jewels in the rubble of the foundations. The hidden wealth in poetry might be a feeling of being more intensely alive, feeling the longing more clearly and sharply. A man told me once that when that happens, you have a chance for a friendship with someone as wildly alive as Shams Tabrizi.

•••••••••••

What is something you're secretly proud you did?

David Huddle: I have a long list of things I'm ashamed of from my high school and college days but almost nothing that I'm proud of, secretly or otherwise. Probably that's why I've written so much about that time in my life—and I still go back to it almost involuntarily. Lots of reckoning and revising to be done. Mostly I just think I was lucky that I didn't get beaten half to death or thrown in jail. I'd say I'm proud I learned how to write pretty good sentences and paragraphs, but more credit for that goes to

Arraga Young, my high school English teacher, than it does to me. Okay, okay, here's something I'm proud of: I spent a lot of time around my grandfather, Charles R. Huddle, Senior, and therefore learned a lot about storytelling and about appreciating "characters" and the situations of their lives. I did that for no other reason than that he kept me interested hour after hour, but at least I had sense enough to sit still and pay attention to him. And ditto Muncy Webb—the railroad stationmaster in my hometown of Ivanhoe, back in the fifties. I'm proud of having somehow realized the value of being in the presence of those men.

··········

You have said that the Flower Garland Sutra has some of your favorite descriptions of our world. Will you recite or paraphrase a favorite?

David Rutschman: I could pretty happily talk about the Avatamsaka Sutra all day long. It's a text that's just . . . I believe the religious studies term is *bonkers*. I mean that in the most reverent sense. It's also a text that's really hard to quote from or paraphrase because it's nearly impossible to capture the scale and intricacy of it. In Thomas Cleary's English translation, it runs over 1500 pages. It just goes on and on and on.

I'll give it a try, though. The sutra offers a vision of reality as containing an infinite number of interpenetrating realms, and there are various places in the text that are simply long, long lists of worlds. What's moving for me isn't so much the description of our world (which uses a standard set of symbols which would take a while to unpack) but more how that description is folded into the rest.

The list of worlds begins like this:

> Above this, past worlds as numerous as atoms in a buddha-field, is a world called Beautiful Array of Lotus Flowers of Various Scents, bounded by all kinds of ornaments, resting on a network of jewel lotus blossoms, shaped like a lion throne, covered with nets of pearls of the colors of all jewels, surrounded by as many worlds as atoms in two buddha-fields. The Buddha is called Supreme Radiance of Lion Light.

The list continues in precisely this format: a few sentences' description of each world, using these standard images of flowers and jewels and nets and so on, then the name of the Buddha for that world, then the next paragraph.

A few pages later, we get:

> Above this, past worlds as many as atoms in a buddha-field, we come to this world, called Endurance, bounded by ornaments of diamonds, held by atmospheres of various colors, resting on a network of lotus flowers, shaped like space, covered by space adorned with spherical celestial palaces, surrounded by worlds as numerous as atoms in thirteen buddha-fields. The Buddha is this *Vairocana*.

Amy, that's us! That's our world! Shaped like space! *Endurance* is how Cleary renders the Sanskrit word *saha*.

Then—this is the best part, the part that gives me goosebumps every time—the list goes on, just like that, world after world, for thirty more pages. We're just one small entry among hundreds. One tiny shard of glass in the kaleidoscope.

••••··•••••••

There is a scene in *Cavedweller* when one of the main characters, Cissy, helps fellow spelunkers out of the cave where they've gotten lost and exhausted themselves. She keeps pulling while they curse her, which seems a distinctly working-class strength.

Dorothy Allison: Yes, and it comes from having some terrible experiences. You learn to trust yourself. A sense of humor also helps.

It was shocking to me—because I was always fascinated with the upper class and dated a lot of girls from the upper class—that they were just so ineffectual. If they got a flat tire, they didn't know how to deal with it. If someone called them a name in the street they didn't know how to respond. They didn't really have a sense of themselves. They didn't have resilience. I've seen in my own family and in my own life you can be pushed to the wall, then take a deep breath and stand up anyway. I don't think everybody learns that, so it's one of the backhanded advantages of having been pushed to the wall so many times.

I'm always conscious of having been the child I was. The

defining moment of my childhood wasn't having been beaten or raped, but of fighting with my sisters over who had to sleep next to the bedroom door (most accessible to our stepfather). That's a degree and caliber of shame that is bone-deep. I will never be able to forgive myself for it. I was the oldest girl and the biggest, and I'd already been raped, and I'd already been beaten, and I knew I could survive it. My sisters were both younger and more fragile, but there were nights when I just couldn't take their place, and because I was bigger and meaner I would not be by the door.

I'm about to be sixty-eight years old. That started when I was six, so that consciousness of responsibility and shame is always present. It's in my writing always. When I give you my characters, there's always somewhere where they're not heroic. They've always got some place where they failed themselves or the ones they love.

....

But what a standard to hold yourself to at six!

Dorothy Allison: Well, being raised in the Baptist church will give you a high standard, but you don't think that way as a six-year-old. You think of yourself as strong. You don't think of yourself as destroyed until you are destroyed. I can't even tell you how many times we fought over who would be near the door. It may have been only once, but it was enough to have marked me, to discover in myself that I was that terrified and desperate.

....

In your Creative Matters talk at the University of Iowa, you suggest that our cultural obsession with covering up scars, wounds, and blemishes limits our ability to interact with each other. Do you see exposure, vulnerability, damage, and recovery as integral to relationship?

Wendy S. Walters: There is no neutral body. Or rather, all bodies are neutral if any one body is. The presumption that anyone might get through life without experiencing damage is narrow-sighted and also, possibly, dangerous to others. As for relationship, it's something that is very important to me—my marriage, my parenting, my extended family, my friendships, my collaborations. I work at all of these. I really like how you framed this question—maybe I'll say damage, vulnerability, exposure, etc. are not integral to relationship, but, rather, that they are inevitable aspects of it.

....

For your essay "Lonely in America," you were moved to research the scattered bones of enslaved Africans when they surfaced during construction at an intersection in Portsmouth, New Hampshire. Your title suggests the loneliness of this knowledge, which exposed a front unified in denying and deflecting responsibility for the institution of slavery. I recount this essay to demonstrate that I am listening, as are many others, but I wonder if writing it made you feel less or more alone?

Wendy S. Walters: My loneliness during the time I was writing that essay came from being around people who refused to acknowledge the impact of slavery and colonialism on contemporary lives. Where did those people live? They weren't in my world. Likewise, I have struggled with being in conversation with those who claim to be anti-racist despite consistently and unequivocally practicing anti-Blackness. What am I supposed to do with that kind of contradiction? It is better to be alone than embrace that.

Because there are children and parents separated from each other in those Texas-border detention camps, indigenous women disappearing all over North America, Black trans women murdered with alarming targeted frequency, and people being contracted to work in prisons without their individual consent, it is increasingly hard for me to think about this history as separate from our present moment. That so many people are beginning to see the connections between these violences is a gift, and it makes the possibility of new narratives more likely.

···········

How did your identity as a Native person shape your sense of self?

Philanese Slaughter: It was odd for me to have been taught that the Creator would always take care of *my* needs. I have spent seventy-three years asking why the self is held in such high regard. For me, the community is always more important than the individual. That's a pretty different lens onto the world. It's doing the thanksgiving offerings, every morning.

When I was about ten years old, my grandfather and I were watering the horses. He was carrying a bucket of water, and I was being a brat, a typical, self-centered kid. "Come over here and put your hand in that bucket of water," he said, so I did. "Little girl," he said, "you are as important as the hole that will be left when you pull out your hand."

••••••••••

That's beautiful.

Philanese Slaughter: It is, and my grandfather only went to school through the third grade. What a demonstration that I was not the center of the universe I thought I was. Yet it wasn't cruel.

My grandfather also never answered questions but always returned a question with a question, because he wanted me to think things through myself.

••••••••••

Did you ever get pulled back into the illusion of self-importance, perhaps as a teenager, when most Americans prize their individuality?

Philanese Slaughter: No, I felt too far outside that experience. American teenagers just seemed weird to me, after having lived abroad for so long. And I didn't understand the white world in general. I didn't know that I didn't understand it; I just didn't know why people thought the way they did. It's hard for a child or an adolescent to intellectualize that kind of disconnect, so instead I headed for the woods and streams. I read books. I gravitated to marginalized groups.

Which led to my most painful experiences of prejudice. At the University of Oklahoma, there were only seven of us—including undergraduates and graduates—who participated in their first graduation of Native Americans. Now, Oklahoma was difficult for Indians, but that's where my husband's job was. Other Natives had tried but left before they graduated, often after their freshmen year. This helped me to become active in the community there. I studied American Indian law. We organized events at the Jim Thorpe building. We boycotted our Masters' graduation ceremony. Actually, we showed up in traditional dress instead of caps and gowns, but they wouldn't let us in. That hurt. It's probably why I became a librarian, so I could help others help themselves.

•••••••••••

When in your life have you felt the freest?

Philanese Slaughter: On horseback. In England, in California, in the Midwest—any time I was on the back of a horse, I felt free.

··········

How did your relationship to nature form?

Raven Jackson: One of my earliest memories is of splitting a fat worm in two for my father as we fished on the edge of the Cumberland River. I remember dirt under my nails, my feet. I remember the dark whiskers of the catfish we caught. I think I fell in love with nature then. Fishing opened the door for me.

As a photographer, I'm particularly interested in taking photos of Black bodies in natural environments. Breathing. Existing. Taking up space. In my poetry and films, I tend to have imagery of fishing, trees, and fields. Rain. These are some of my obsessions. For instance, in my poem "all dirt roads taste of salt," which became the title of my feature film project, I write: "winter: the trees won't stop screaming / i put on a dress i've lost the buttons to, refuse / to stay home."

In the feature film I'm currently writing, my protagonist has a strong relationship with rain—it reminds her of her mother who passed away when she was young. The water cycle of rain is an image I find myself returning to often. For me, how rain changes form is reminiscent of how energy changes form. There's something deeply powerful in writing a character that swallowed rain as a child and, as an adult, emotionally connects with her mother in the drops.

··········

When in your life have you felt the freest?

Ira Sukrungruang: I love snorkeling. I lose myself in this underwater world. I don't feel my body. I float and follow, and once it got me into trouble because I was so far from shore, carried away into the belly of the ocean by a rip tide. I survived, barely. Still, I go back. That calm, the change in sound, the change in body . . . I don't know, it's easy to lose yourself because in a weird way there is no self. It's like what Ted Kooser said once about a good poem: an enchantment happens, and it's like staring at the bottom of a glass-bottom boat, and you lose yourself and keep leaning in and leaning in until your head hits the glass and the spell is broken. Coming up in snorkeling is that shock back.

IX.

Going Past the Skin into Another Skin

MY MOTHER'S MOTHER saved fabric for quilts: flannel shirts her boys had outgrown, her daughters' cotton nightgowns, denim her husband had worn soft, scraps bagged and sold for a penny at yard sales. Her two favorite patterns for these color blocks were bow ties and Dutch dolls. She had quilts in progress until the day she died, and baskets overflowing with starts in various stages of completion. While she stitched, I sat on the floor and sandwiched stacks of gaberdine, corduroy, poplin, chenille, lace, and cotton, mixing and matching colors to mimic layers of hamburger, pimento cheese, etc., which flopped and sagged when I pretended to bite into them like the words to which they belonged. The textures of both delighted me.

I slept under quilts, had fever dreams when sick with the flu and starry-eyed daydreams when swooning into love, under patchwork patterns that gave me the sense everything that had ever been would turn up again in some other form. My family didn't believe in reincarnation, but reincarnated objects surrounded us. Old tires became tree swings. Clawfoot bathtubs were repurposed as feed troughs. My grandfather saved baler twine, which he used to fasten everything from cattle gates to tailgates. My mother saved paper bags, buttons, and wood from fallen trees on the farm to make our mantel board, coffee table, and picture frames. My grandmother converted chipped plates into plant saucers, collaged broken glass into tabletop mosaics. And my father did his part by wearing new T-shirts to the field as soon as possible, so they became fit for what my mother called the rag bag. I learned to dust using my own cotton diaper cloths.

Inevitably, I began to save conversations that mattered, once I came to value them in Rhonda Simmerman's ninth-grade English class. Material, we called it, on the newspaper staff in college.

Daily, spiders eat their webs to recoup the energy expended to spin them, but if the spider outside my window made her way to the ground after the rain to salvage the waste of her enormous web, I didn't see her. The next morning, though, I did see a strand glistening across the gulf she had bridged the previous day. At first, I thought that anchor alone remained unbroken by the storm, but no, she had managed it again. Over the next hour she wove a new web just as wide and bold as her first. It shone gold, blue, ruby red, and green with dew in the sunlight.

"If a job is worth doing, it's worth doing right," my grandmother used to say, according to my mother, who had to repeat many of my Granny Johnstone's lessons since she died when I was seven. Mom often told the story while we washed dishes of the time her mother had found a dirty plate, flecked with food, and unloaded every other washed dish from the drainer and made her three girls start over. She threatened to do the same to my brother and me but never did, though I remember the adage when considering the spider's determination. How could she know this location and span would be worth so much of her life's effort? I marveled at her daring or trust, innocent as a daisy in a football stadium parking lot, its petals uplifted to the sun as if in a meadow, expectant that any minute a pollinating bee would come along.

Albert Einstein says that the "first and most basic question all people must answer for themselves" is whether the universe is a friendly place. Do you think the universe is a friendly place?

Marc Gaba: I think that in the final analysis, whatever that is, I'll say yes despite my no. See, the universe is just what it is, that's all, and it really is what the word *all* could refer to, don't you think? I find it impossible to think in a metaphor that is also a personification. The rhetoric fails, because the *friend* in *friendly* calls to mind specific people that I neither mistake nor idealize, and my failure to mistake and idealize them is what I would say is love. But to entertain the metaphor, I would say the universe is not so much friendly as loving. I would like to think that critiquing is a function of care; our skeptical age would be so meaningless otherwise.

•··········••

In your essay "On Recuperation," you quote Walt Whitman's "Those who love each other shall become invincible." Will you elaborate on how you read this line?

Stephen J. West: I think that line suggests the intimacy Whitman demands from his readers, but the attempt at intimacy doesn't end with the words on the page. It's almost like he's expecting a reader to have an actual personal connection with him through reading his lines—not just with the ideas, or the language. That's all there too, but he wants more. It's intense. If Whitman ever felt betrayed by readers—and this poem says he did—I think it's because the level of intimacy he offered could never be reciprocated, as in a relationship that's doomed to fail because one person is light years farther into it than the other.

··········

You include four essays on neighbors in *Stealing History*, as well as a number of anecdotes about neighbors—including my favorites, Charlie, a former member of the World War II Signal Corps, and his incontinent dog Elvira. Your interest in them connects to your narrative along a thread so fine it illustrates the invisible tug of connection between people. I gather you don't confine neighborhoods to next-door relations, but what quality of mutuality prompts you to claim someone as your neighbor?

Gerald Stern: I have the oddest neighbors. Ovid, Blake, the Greek poets, Apollinaire, my next-door neighbor's mother-in-law from Holland, Irene from across the street who has been advising me on my garden, and all the people I meet through my walks and conversations in this small city.

Charlie, whom I write about in three separate sections in *Stealing History*, has become a close friend. He has lived, for twenty-seven years, in a very tiny, somewhat dark, but nonetheless pleasant apartment, at the rear of a house. He spends most of the day listening to music and playing his recorder. He still loves to talk about his own life and, as I indicated in the book, he has replaced Elvira with a frisky, younger dog. He is a little bent over, and certainly smaller than he once was. A lovely woman in town—who was his lover twenty or thirty years ago—told me that he was tall, slim, and the handsomest man she had ever met.

In my backyard, walking onto the towpath beside the canal, I saw suddenly last night a collection of eight or ten people and four or five dogs. I knew some of them, but they all knew me. I claim them as neighbors. Certainly, you are my neighbor. I would never want to be a neighbor with Romney. He would steal me blind.

•••••••••••

Do you collect anything?

David Iacovazzi-Pau: I'm not a collector of things. My interest lies more in the people I meet and the places I travel. On one of my trips out west I took a Greyhound bus and met a musician from Austin, Texas. Since he was sitting next to me, we started to talk. He asked me what I was looking for out there, and I told him, "I'm looking for colors."

•••••••••••

Your current project researches the history and use of white paint. Will you tell me more about it?

Wendy S. Walters: This project came out of my personal obsession with rooms painted in white. The piece started one fall when I was complaining to another parent at my son's school about the freshly covered walls. She thought I was being ridiculous. The school looked so much better than it had the previous spring. But I didn't feel right about the color—about children learning in a space that was so bright, so reflective.

The project brings together my personal, aesthetic, and creative interests in design in a new way. The drafts I have of the early chapters are still very much in progress. My hope is that this project will change the way people talk about color in space, especially in cultural and educational institutions. By thinking about color in rooms where significant learning and social decisions are made, we might develop a more nuanced understanding of our relationship to creative production. I am really interested in the way design and nonfiction might intersect in method, how together they might reveal new formal opportunities.

In addition to that, I am writing a book about the industrial Midwest, with an eye to how the Black middle class fit(s) into that space. I am interested in the aesthetics of class experience, and the ways that industrial backdrop shapes perceptions of power and beauty.

....

How has looking at multiple generations informed your story?

Rebecca McClanahan: In *The Tribal Knot*, the memoir part—my own story—is most present at the beginning of the book and then in the last few chapters, though bits of personal memoir surface every now and then in the ancestral history that spans about 120 years. In the first several years of writing the book, I tried to keep my own story out, period. I'd envisioned *The Tribal Knot* as more of a group biography of my ancestors. I would be their biographer, braiding their stories together. Life, as usual, had other plans: I got ambushed by their stories. The relatives and ancestors, living and dead, found me out, cornered me. "Come on out, you coward," they seemed to say. "You're part of this family too!" Turns out, I needed their stories to understand my own life. Their lives had formed me, for better or worse, and I needed to claim these lives as my own, as I hope my ancestors and descendants would want to claim mine.

•••‧‧•‧‧••‧‧

You use a painting technique known as underpainting, which is a process of laying down color on a canvas at the outset rather than beginning to paint from a blank slate. Does this method of creating an instant palimpsest make the initial layer less willful than ones that follow?

Sheep Jones: Yes. The first layer, which is a transparent glaze, is less willful. I used to mix an earth orange with ultramarine blue, but lately I have been more daring, using phthalo blue or permanent rose. The next layer consists of patches of opaque areas, building up the various segments that I want isolated. What happens is, that initial transparent color sets the tone of the painting and shimmers throughout the end result.

•••••••••••

In your introduction to *The Story About the Story: Great Writers Explore Great Literature,* you include Walter Kirn's claim that the mark of a great book is not its staying power but its dissolution into the waft of curtains when the scenes change. I wonder if you know the poet Tan Lin, because Kirn's sentiment reminds me of Lin's question: "What is it like to eat an idea or its suggestion? As anyone who has eaten can tell you, the most beautiful memories are memories that one has forgotten how to have."

J. C. Hallman: We often say that every time we read an admired book we find something new in it. If in saying this we're not suggesting that somehow new material has crept into the book since the last time we looked at it, then the implication is that somehow when we read we are imperfect receivers, and we don't get "all" of it each time we read it. But what if this is wrong? What if it's wrong to think of meaning quantitatively like that? What seems more likely is that the thing that has changed is us—the reader. We see "new" things because we, in fact, are new when we return to a book. I think this is what Kirn—and, I'm guessing, Tan Lin, whom I've not read—is getting at. In a sense, as we grow and learn, we "forget" our old selves. The new self, then, can enjoy old pleasures—food, stories—on more than one level: as a recollection, a rereading, and a fresh experience for the new self, a self that is now equipped to appreciate that experience differently.

············

Like you, the artist Kiki Smith expresses an interest in boundaries, at one point describing the skin as an envelope. You similarly suggest that fantasy is one way we negotiate hard and fast divisions. How would you say the imagination shifts or transforms boundaries?

Nicole Walker: Fantasy or the imagination doesn't come like TV. It is not witnessed; it's accessed. The idea of an envelope is close, but I see imagination as the outing of the inside, of going past the skin into another skin. The energy to get you there comes from an internal place, but when it catapults you out, that is really being. It's as if you have become a tree and now carbon dioxide is what you breathe instead of oxygen—and here again, you're living twice.

············

Years ago, my parents bought a pasture bordered by a creek, groves of walnut trees, and a high limestone bluff that creates a feeling of privacy. We call it the Meadow, which is why I share the image with you—because you write that *meadow* is the word you most love in the English language. What is the word you love second-most?

Gerald Stern: I think my second favorite word in the English language is *blue*, the color blue; but when I think of blue, I am really thinking more of a kind of lavender. As I understand it, blue is the color of death in Egyptian mythology and culture, as it is the color of life in Jewish culture and mythology. Mary, mother of Jesus, is represented by the color blue. Miriam and Mary have their root in the word *bitterness*, or *salty*, which relates to the sea, which is also blue as we envision it. My favorite meadow was in Clarion County in northwestern Pennsylvania. It was also contained and isolated, as yours is. I remember there being two flowers in that meadow; one of them was daisies, but I can't remember the other. Several times I slept in that meadow for hours, staring up at the blue sky. I guess it was heaven.

....

We know our own wells of desire to be bottomless, but have you seen someone else's, for a memorable moment, fill?

Nicole Walker: My friend Misty, who grapples up Eagle Creek in Portland with her bare hands, who works in immigration law, whose daughter eats forty-seven Cuties a day, who grows tomatoes even in Portland's half-assed sun, seems almost always satisfied. I am in awe of her belief in the full moment. My friend Rebecca, whose daughter has been in the hospital for four months learning how to breathe—the moment (and it was just a moment, before the anxiety set in) when I got to overhear the nurse say they were taking the daughter off the jet ventilator...*that* was full. Also, my daughter when she does math.

......·····..

When, and how, do you feel fulfilled as a writer, if you do?

Jane Tompkins: I used to write because I needed to get ahead professionally, because I had something to say that I really wanted people to hear, and because I wanted to prove something to myself. Eventually, after an embarrassingly long time, I realized I was ambitious. I also wrote because I enjoyed the creative process, although that came in third. Now, I'd say, it comes first. The pleasure of the process is a high, exhilarating and absorbing. Makes me want to smoke—which I do sometimes, a small cigar, at the contemplation stage. Right now, I'm in a period where I see pictures everywhere and want to paint them all. I think the shift from product to process is important because it keeps you alive.

In watercolor painting, accident plays a role, the uncontrolled blending of colors, the accidental line, the blur, the mistake. The process is spontaneous (at least, the way I paint it is) and has to take place quickly, before the water dries. This accidental quality, which contributes so much to the effects of watercolor, is not something I've encountered in writing. There, I have no sense of the role of random occurrences in the shaping of a composition. Maybe I need to get back to pure freewriting, which is close to stream of consciousness, in order to approximate the random elements that I'm talking about. But I'm not sure that chance plays, or can play, the same role in writing as in watercolors. (I'm excluding oils, and other media where you can go back over things and fix them in a way that watercolors don't allow.) The happenstance part of watercolors is what I want to emphasize more. What I don't like about a lot of my paintings is the impression they give of being too controlled (not that I have that much control, mind you, I'm just talking about an overall effect).

For some reason, this question reminds me of something a young writer told me years ago. She was a North Carolinian who spent lots of time in nature. She talked about just "being with" the river, or the forest. Maybe that wasn't even the way she said it. It's like the line from Robert Frost: "He thought he kept the universe alone." The idea of "keeping" nature just by being there, in it, with it, is the aspect of writing that intrigues me now—the being with it, the doing of it for the sake of doing it. I feel enormously lucky to have arrived at a place where I can "keep" the world by writing or painting a watercolor. But at the same time I wonder if this is as good a way to spend time as doing volunteer work. Does my doing another watercolor that hardly anyone will see help the world? It does so simply by being in harmony with it. It does so by adding to the world's quotient of happiness. It's seeing yourself as part of the world you are endeavoring to "improve," and doing so by allowing yourself to be happily absorbed in it and by it.

・・・・・・・・・・・

When in your life have you felt the freest?

David Huddle: It's a relatively recent discovery—of, say, the last four or five years. I photograph birds, and mostly the ones to come to my backyard in Burlington, Vermont. Mostly the usual suspects—chickadees, sparrows, juncos, blue jays, cardinals, woodpeckers, finches, crows, grackles, and sometimes there are occasional appearances of wrens and titmice. I sit in front of French doors that look out on trees, plants, a fountain, and bird feeders, and if I wish, I can sit still and capture moments with my camera when the birds are doing what they do. I don't try for those calendar photos when the birds seem to strike exactly the right pose. I'm more interested in their usual behavior with its odd antics and habits.

I particularly enjoy photographing them when they're interacting with other birds, whether of their own kind or of a different species. I like to catch them fighting, but I also like to photograph pairs of them sticking together—the male cardinal sometimes will feed his mate a seed as (in my opinion) a courting gift, and I can't resist taking that picture whenever it is available.

What does photographing birds have to do with feeling free? When I'm engaged in trying to take a picture of a certain kind of bird, I completely escape myself. Or I am free of every thought and sensation except those having to do with focusing on that bird and snapping the shutter at the right moment. And in that focusing on what its next move might be, my consciousness becomes more that of a bird than of a human being.

During the migration season, warblers, orioles, vireos, buntings, cedar waxwings, and tanagers pass through our backyard garden—not all at once, but frequently enough that I can become completely engaged in the mission of taking pictures of these rare visitors for as much as an hour at a time. The rarer the bird, it seems to me, the more quickly they dart from one place to another and exercise their skill at hiding in hedges, among tree limbs, anywhere but out in the open. In the attempt to photograph these shy and wily creatures, I'm alert and focused in a way that I never am in any other aspect of my life. I don't even think of looking at my phone, my watch, or my computer. I automatically give up all of my usual concerns—which is to say that the self disappears or dissolves for long, beautiful swatches of time. For that fraction of my lifetime, I am granted the great privilege of disappearing into the cosmos.

....

"It is not a given," you write, "that the heart is lonely and so must live forever." What *is* a given?

David Keplinger: Nothing is given. Nothing is certain; even Newton's physics break down at the subatomic level. Nothing is promised from my human perspective. From my animal perspective, I think everything is given—everything is still here, right now, good for the taking, a gift.

....

In your essay "My Listening Was Mumbling," you say about the writing process that "there is something spiritual about the endeavor . . . in the sense that you're constantly made humble because you're reminded you can't take credit for these origins." Will you elaborate on that humility?

Bob Hicok: How to put this? Walking around, eating a sandwich, listening to a bird, talking to my wife, picking my nose—I have almost no belief in myself as a writer. It's just not there. I know it's supposed to be, and that many hold the notion that you can't write (or paint or make excellent snow cones) if you don't have faith in your abilities. But again, away from the act of writing, I don't see myself as anything special. And it's not that I see myself as special while I write—more that I don't see myself at all. There is a disappearance into the act, into the desire or need to speak, that erases—I mean, completely obliterates—the doubts and personal bullshit that tools around with me. Doing becomes being. Plain and simple, or fancy and, I guess, not so. And because of this, I begin most days having quieted my most cannibalistic tendencies. So yeah—give me that gift every day and I'll treat it with respect and humility. And I give it all the coffee it wants.

•••••••••••

You have a line in a story about a hog that has just survived a dire situation that two of his friends have not. The hog questions whether he feels grateful and answers himself by saying: "It was hard to say, so hard to sum it all up, to keep it from turning into something else." Is there a pause before each moment turns into something else, which writing helps you recognize?

David Rutschman: I appreciate you highlighting that sentence. There is a kind of rush in our experience, I think—how I'm always turning into something else, how the world is always turning into something else—and also the possibility of a kind of pause.

And it's the *relationship* between the two that's most moving to me. The way the pause blooms in the rush, the way the rush swells up in the pause.

My entire life feels like it takes place right there in that inter-play, actually, that back and forth. Maybe yours does too. Maybe that's where we can all find each other.

•••••••••••

Do you consider literature to be an alternate form of gospel?

Dorothy Allison: It's all glory at a distance from the mundane, and the mundane is mere survival. Gospel music, like poetry, like great literature, is glory. I'm reaching for glory. I wanted to live forever. I still do, but I have a much more complicated relationship to death than when I was younger. I am more accepting now. I no longer have that overwhelming impulse to live forever, but that's the impulse that makes art. That's the secret desire—that and the desire to separate yourself from those who hold you in contempt, whether that's your stepfather or your cousins or your church or people at the grammar school who made you take an IQ test again. You want to claim your right to be among not just the humans but among the best of them.

ACKNOWLEDGMENTS

Edited excerpts originally appeared as interviews in the following publications: *elimae*, *Guernica*, *Kenyon Review Online*, *Literary Orphans*, *New Orleans Review*, *Southern Cultures*, *The Writer*, and *Zone 3*.

A lengthy essay from this manuscript was originally published in the *Georgia Review* as "I Knew Some of Them, But They All Knew Me."

This book would not exist without the wisdom and dynamism of the contributors featured in these pages. I am so grateful to each of you for sharing your perspectives with me, often over spans of years. Especial thanks to David Huddle, whose literary reading in our shared hometown convinced me at age eleven that literature could rise as well from Appalachia as from London. To him, I sent the first draft of the long essay that began this conversation. If he had not recognized its originality, it would have gone the way of so many other incomparable experiments. Deep thanks to Stephen Corey, who validated this outlier with publication in the *Georgia Review* and provided spot-on edits to the final manuscript.

The lion's share of these interviews first appeared in the journal *Zone 3*, so I extend my gratitude to fellow editors Aubrey Collins,

Stephanie Dugger, Blas Falconer (emeritus), Barry Kitterman, Andrea Spofford, and Susan Wallace (emeritus) for the flexibility to ask field-crossing questions.

Thank you also to Department Chair Dr. Mercy Cannon, Dean of the College of Arts and Letters Barry Jones, my fellow faculty members, and the administration of Austin Peay State University, for fellowship opportunities and travel funds to conduct much of the field research included here.

This reticent farm girl would never have raised her voice without the encouragement and support of so many others, including Ericka Arcadia, David Baker, Terry Banker, Dan Corrie, Bob and Beto Cumming, Mechele Felts, Kate Glasgow, Lee Gray, Joanne Greenberg, Joey Grisham, Helen Johnstone (in memoriam), Geeta Kothari, Eric LeMay, Amelia Martens, Michael Martone, Dinty W. Moore, Janisse Ray, Martin Riker, Don Sudbrink, Joni Tevis, Nicole Walker, Amanda Winfree, Janet Wright, Randy Wright, and Jeremy Wright (in memoriam).

Finally, without the recognition and support of Sarah Gorham and Sarabande Books, it might never have seemed worth it— every effort and failed effort to formulate the right question, to reach beyond my own experiences to educate myself, and to claim my right to be among such people. Thank you.

AMY WRIGHT has previously authored two poetry books and six chapbooks. Her essays have won contests sponsored by *London Magazine* and *Quarterly West*. She has also received two Peter Taylor Fellowships to The *Kenyon Review* Writers Workshop, an Individual Artist Fellowship from the Tennessee Arts Commission, and a fellowship to Virginia Center for the Creative Arts. Her essays appear in *Brevity, Fourth Genre, Georgia Review, Kenyon Review, Ninth Letter,* and elsewhere.

SARABANDE BOOKS is a nonprofit literary press located in Louisville, KY. Founded in 1994 to champion poetry, short fiction, and essay, we are committed to creating lasting editions that honor exceptional writing. For more information, please visit sarabandebooks.org.